To Hunt, Shoot and Stalk

(Hunting and conservation tales of an Irish Sportsman at home and in the U.S.)

by John Lalor

©MAYFLY LODGE PUBLISHING
Cahir, Co. Tipperary, Ireland
2000

e-mail: jlalor@operamail.com

I.S.B.N. 0-9538499-0-2

Design & Print by:
Kilkenny People Printing Ltd., Kilkenny, Ireland

Published by:
Mayfly Lodge Publishing

Dedicated to
Maria and Aoife

Best Wishes

John Falen

Ballywalter

CONTENTS

To Hunt, Shoot and Stalk

INTRODUCTION ....Page 7
FOREWORD (By Dr. Douglas Butler)..Page 8
ACKNOWLEDGEMENTS ....Page 10

- CHAPTER 1: Red Grouse ....Page 11
- CHAPTER 2: September Mallard ....Page 15
- CHAPTER 3: Pheasant ....Page 19
- CHAPTER 4: Fallow in the Rut...Page 26
- CHAPTER 5: Crop Protection - Pigeons and Crows ....Page 33
- CHAPTER 6: Ferrets and Ferreting..................................Page 36
- CHAPTER 7: Driven Pheasants ....Page 39
- CHAPTER 8: Fox Hunting..Page 45
- CHAPTER 9: Sika Deer in Wicklow ....Page 52
- CHAPTER 10: Timber Doodles and Woodcock...................Page 55
- CHAPTER 11: Black Bear in Maine ....Page 60
- CHAPTER 12: Whitetail Deer ....Page 68
- CHAPTER 13: Flighting Canada Geese ....Page 76
- CHAPTER 14: Bobcat ....Page 82
- CHAPTER 15: Red Deer Stalking in Scotland ....Page 91
- CHAPTER 16: Clay Pigeon Shooting - The Flapper Shoot ....Page 98
- CHAPTER 17: Ruffed Grouse ....Page 104
- CHAPTER 18: Wild Turkey ....Page 109
- CHAPTER 19: Black Bear from a Tree Stand ....Page 113
- CHAPTER 20: Dogs ....Page 118
- CHAPTER 21: Firearm Legislation....................................Page 122

BIBLIOGRAPHY ....Page 128

Introduction

The sport of hunting is one of the most ancient pastimes in our Irish heritage and history. The Fianna were an ancient group of Irish legendary warriors who spent half of the year hunting red deer. Oisín, the son of Fionn MacCumhaill, was hunting red deer near the lakes of Killarney when he encountered Niamh Cinn Ór, beautiful princess who came from Tír na nÓg, better known as the Land of Eternal Youth.

Shooting, hunting, stalking and game fishing, were the sports of the privileged in Ireland up to the beginning of this century (twentieth). The wealthy landlords controlled and owned the hunting and shooting rights. Woe betide the poor peasant who was caught poaching a pheasant, deer or salmon. Many Australians of Irish decent can trace their ancestors back to the prison ships 'waiting in the harbour'. There was a great change in the ownership of land in Ireland between 1880 and the 1930's. Many of the large estates were divided among smaller landowners, by means of the Land Acts. Some of the rights to game hunting and fishing were transferred at the same time or bought out at a later date.

As a result of this great change, many people took up shooting, hunting and fishing as a pastime. The working week has been reduced to five days in most instances, and this provides more people with greater leisure opportunities. Men, women and children take part in the various aspects of field sports today and the number is steadily increasing as we enter the new millennium.

The purpose of this book is to provide information for the hunter about hunting and conservation in Ireland and the U.S. today. It will be invaluable for the beginner, a good book to relax with when the season is over or when time and family circumstances do not allow a trip to the Great Outdoors.

Foreword

Few things are more deeply entwined in the fabric of rural Ireland than field sports. According to the season, there are those who seek the magic of woodcock springing from frost shrouded bracken, red grouse tearing from purple flowered heather, or brown trout splashing lazily on a sultry summer's evening.

Some have a first and only love. Around ten percent of Irish game shooters will hunt nothing save that gaudy alien from the Far East, the cock pheasant.

Others, driven by some primeval programming, seek each quarry in its time. For such hunters, there are days which pose a delicious dilemma. September 1st is a case in point. At daybreak will he wait in ambush for those first flocks of greedy mallard circling golden barley stubbles. Or will he, puffing furiously after a tough uphill climb, set out across the heather in pursuit of grouse?

Field sports know not national boundaries. The excitement of the chase is the same everywhere ... only the ingredients differ. The ruffed grouse of the prairies produces for the American hunter, the same spurt of adrenalin that the red grouse provides for his Irish counterpart.

And the affection and esteem which all hunters have for their quarry is equal too ... something our anti 'friends' simply cannot understand.

Well over two hundred thousand people are involved in field sports in the Republic. Yet, strangely, books about hunting, shooting or fishing here are comparatively rare. Of former eras, there are, indeed, a number of classics. But, of the present, there is very little. In this book, therefore, John makes a valuable and long overdue contribution to the world of Irish field sports.

At heart we are a nation of rough shooters and, chapter by chapter, we are taken through the joys and sometimes sorrows, of the hunting field. Taken on these trips in a way that only a hunter can describe.

Contrary to popular opinion, success and failure are not measured in terms of the size of the bag. As John takes us through days in Ireland and the United States, he reveals all those things that contribute to a great day's hunting ... wild surroundings, lonesome places, good companionship, questing dogs, setters frozen on the quarry, springers tearing through heavy cover like so many miniature elephants, ducks silhouetted against a darkening sky.

And across the Atlantic, where he had the good fortune to roam, another hunting world, another set of traditions.

TO HUNT, SHOOT and STALK is the first of a new generation of Irish sporting books. John must be complimented in pioneering this particular trail. Sharing one's experiences with others is no small part of the enjoyment of hunting.

I look forward to Volume 2.

Douglas Butler

Acknowledgements

The following people and organisations are due a great deal of gratitude in helping me to write and publish this book.

Mr. Des Crofton, Director of the N.A.R.G.C., Mr. Frederick McGolderick who helped me with all the details on clay-pigeon shooting.

Mr. Donal Barrett for awakening my interest in ferrets.

Mary and Billy O'Regan of the Southern Deer Society.

Mr. Mike MacEwan for all his time and help with regard to fox hunting.

Mr. Mark Carver of Secret Pond Camps, Patten, Maine, U.S.A. who taught me about the wildlife and the techniques of American hunting.

Jared White who gave instruction on goose decoying and 'calling' wild turkeys.

Mr. Michael Phelan (R.I.P.) of the Shelton Driven Pheasant Shoot.

Garda Tomás MacMahon, Firearms Instructor, Garda Training College, Templemore and detective Mark O'Meara, Cahir. Mr. Sean Breen, Wildlife Ranger, South Tipperary. Dr. Douglas Butler for his contribution to the Foreward. Fallons for the use of their maps.

Ann Walsh for all her patience and work in typing the manuscript.

Anne Ryan for setting out the manuscript.

My son Shane for his computer graphics.

All the photographers who gave me their prints.

The Ruffed Grouse Society of America, The National Wild Turkey Federation, The National Rifle Association of America and the Royal Ulster Constabulary.

A special word of thanks to all the men and women with whom I have hunted on both sides of the Atlantic Ocean and who are too many to name individually.

Go Raibh Míle Maith Agaibh!

CHAPTER ONE

The Red Grouse

The Red Grouse is a bird, which is rarely seen by anybody except hill walkers and grouse shooters. The bird was always native to Ireland, the Irish name being An Cearc Fraoigh (i.e. the hen of the heather). Grouse are very scarce today and on some mountain ranges they are almost extinct. The main reasons for the decline in their numbers are due to afforestation, burning of heather and overgrazing. A serious problem is the burning of heather at the wrong time of the year when the young chicks are on the ground. Our native grouse is in fact a Willow Grouse in one of its specific colour phases. In the Northern tundra areas of Europe and North America the grouse turns completely white in winter to camouflage itself in the snow.

The Irish Red Grouse has a dark reddish brown plumage just like the grouse in Great Britain. The male and female are similar but the cock is slightly larger and has red combs over the eyes. Their combs become bigger during the breeding season and become a deeper shade of red. Their legs are feathered in grey and white down to the tips of the claws. At one time the claws were set in silver to make a ladies brooch.

The birds weigh between 500 – 700g. They breed after one year and lay from 7 – 11 eggs. The eggs hatch after 22 days and the chicks can fly after two weeks. Their diet consists of the seeds, buds and twigs of heather. They will also eat fruit and insects. They have a very short, slightly curved beak which is extremely strong. Grouse are related to pheasants and partridges – let us hope that the grouse will not meet a fate like our native partridge.

The majority of shooters have heard of the 'Glorious 12th'. This is the 12th August when the grouse season begins on the Grouse Moors in the Highlands of Scotland.. Driven shoots are the main method used and it may cost up to £1000 per day. In other areas you can take your own dogs and have a days walked – up shooting.

The grouse season begins in the Republic of Ireland on the 1st September and ends on the 30th. This causes problems of a minor nature for many outdoor sports people, as there may be good runs of Atlantic salmon and the duck and deer season open on the same date.

As the grouse lives above the tree line a certain amount of exertion or hard walking will be needed. Wellingtons are not suitable for hill walking as they do not support the ankles and are notorious for losing their grip on

Counties of Ireland ... border between the Republic of Ireland and Northern Ireland

wet heather or lichen covered rocks. A pair of very strong boots is essential. They must give a snug fit as a day on the hill will soon find any faults and blisters will make for a very uncomfortable walk. A light waterproof jacket should also be brought in your shooting vest. A cool wet wind can cause wind chill even in the month of September. Every hill walker and mountaineer takes a compass and o.s. map.

The Grouse shooter should at least take a compass and know how to use it. The most experienced people can lose their bearings if a fog comes down suddenly. When we go up the mountain part of our aim is to get away from the hassles of everyday life. We hope to get some peace and quiet and to get a brace of grouse is an added bonus. Mobile phones are best left at home, but on the mountain they can be life-savers in the event of an accident. A phone should be carried but switched off. Our Irish weather is very fickle and it is always best to be prepared for possible mishaps. The ideal dogs for grouse are pointers, setters or H.P.R's. Many hunters use a pair of similar dogs. Spaniels are used for driven grouse but for most Irishmen who hunt in two's an Irish setter, English Setter or Llewellyn seem to be the norm. The gun to use is your standard game gun, 12 or 16 gauge – be it side by side or over and under. The cartridge should be a hunting load in no. 6 and no. 7.

Last September my shooting companions and I went up the Galtee Mountains in Co. Tipperary for two hours in the evening. We had a German shorthaired Pointer, a Llewellyn, an English Pointer and a Brittany Spaniel. We split up into pairs, my friend John and I using the Pointer and the Brittany. There was no wind and it was a nice cool evening for a walk

The first thing we saw was a flock of sheep just above the tree line. When they saw the dogs they fled in the exact direction in which we had hoped to go. Seventy yards out they flushed a covey of seven grouse, which flew for 500 yards and then disappeared over a small knoll. We knew that the birds would be jumpy the next time we approached them so we were prepared for a sudden flush rather than a 'good point'. We were walking about 70 yards apart when John's black and white pointer picked up a hot scent. A bird broke from the heather to John's left and flew back from where we came. However the bird tumbled to the ground forty yards out with one shot from his 26" o/u Franchi 12 Bore. The bird was a hen from this season's brood. We searched hard for the other birds but to no avail. I decided to head for the Crags, as there was always a chance of a bird there. The Crags were 300 yards further on. When we searched the spot we decided to split up and meet on the other side.

'Brandy', my Brittany Spaniel was only ten months old and the first bird he had close contact with was John's before we put it into the game bag. Suddenly he scented a bird and came to point. As I approached a pair of grouse sprung from the ground and began to fly over a ridge about 20 yards out. I fired two shots from my Fabarm Euro Three and saw a floating feather as the birds disappeared over the ridge. Brandy also disappeared and when I reached the top I saw him trying to pick up his first grouse. He brought back a fine old cock with beautiful red combs above his eyes and heavily feathered legs. Things happened so fast that I cannot remember if the cock gave the characteristic 'craak – craak' when he was flying away.

The sun was beginning to set so we decided to head for home. We planned to hunt to the west of the area where we had shot the first bird. The dogs hunted closer to the plantation and we were about 50 yards apart. Both dogs picked up a scent and after a minute both came to point almost simultaneously. As we approached the birds flushed. John missed his bird but I was lucky to down my bird at 45 yards. Another bird broke out of range but went in the direction, which we had to follow to get to the jeeps. We noted where the bird landed but try as we did we found no sign of the bird.

We joined Michael and Niall back at the starting point. They met only one grouse, which flushed out of range. It was now 8p.m. and the light was fading. We had 2 hens and 1 cock in 2 hours. We considered ourselves extremely lucky as to see just one grouse is a thrill for many young sportsmen and sportswomen nowadays.

It is the 13th April as I write this chapter. There is a dusting of snow and a bitter Northwest wind blowing over the Galtees. Some of the remaining birds of the initial covey are probably lying on a nest in the heather at the moment. Hopefully there will be many more coveys to be seen next September.

CHAPTER TWO

September Mallard

It is the middle of July 1999, and the River Suir in County Tipperary is at its lowest level in years due to the dry weather and the heat. The reeds on the banks of the river are high and thick, and the weeds which are growing from the bed of the river are appearing above the surface. There are also some giant rushes protruding from this carpet of weed. This type of environment produces ideal habitat for both fish and waterfowl.

During the weekend I saw three female mallard with their young broods. The first had just two ducklings which looked about three weeks old. Mallard lay on average ten eggs so maybe a mink killed the remainder of the brood. The second mallard had seven in her family and the third had nine. Mallard generally hatch their eggs in May so I think that these three clutches were a second hatch for all three females. This augurs well for the total mallard population as with the lack of floods this summer, a high percentage of birds should survive to the beginning of the season on the 1st September.

The mallard (Anas platyrhynchos) is the most common of our wild duck and it is found almost worldwide, but especially in the northern hemisphere. It was domesticated by the Chinese for eggs, meat and feathers. Indeed drake feathers are very much in demand for making lake flies like the Mallard and Claret. The breast feathers are dyed to make mayflies. In recent years, the French have tied artificial trout flies called Cul-de-Canards. The feathers are taken from the area surrounding the preening gland which is on the duck's back about two inches from its rectum. These feathers make excellent floating flies for dry-fly fishing as they never have to have artificial oils applied.

The mallard is a dabbling duck and can be found in shallow areas unlike diving ducks which are generally found in deeper water where they live on fish. The mallard has little plates on its bill called lamellae which it uses to strain food from the water. However, the mallard is omnivorous and every hunter knows that it can be found just as easily in a dry corn or stubble field in the early autumn. The males differ from the females by their bottle-green glossy heads and neck but both sexes look the same after the breeding season when they begin to moult.

The duck shooting season begins in Ireland on 1st September and ends on 31st January. During the month of August, hunters will have spotted or scouted the areas in which they intend to shoot. At this time of the year duck will be found flighting into corn stubble just after dawn or on shallow river flats in the early morning. At dusk the birds may be flighted at ponds where they come to drink and to avoid predators. Later on in the season, the birds may be shot in bogs, marshes or on flood plains. Storms at sea will drive coastal ducks inland and numbers may also be added to by birds migrating from the continent where the winters are much harsher. Ireland is surrounded by water but it is also warmed by the North Atlantic Drift and the Gulf Stream. This means that the water very seldom freezes here. Mallard often seem scarce and are hard to get during some winters. I find that the answer to this is that there is too much water due to long wet periods and that the ducks have too many places where they feed or flight.

I couldn't go duck shooting on the 1st September last year but the weather was still and balmy on the 2nd, so I decided to go to a double-pond which was one mile from the River Suir and in the middle of lush corn-land. The main pond is in a depression with a high bank and trees on the west side. The edges are covered in reeds and rushes. Ten feet to the North of this is another pond which was formed in recent years due to the high water table. This pond is completely exposed and there is no way of approaching it during daylight hours without being seen by any ducks which may be there already. There are only two or three clumps of rushes at the edges but during the evening flight, it can be an excellent location.

When duck shooting, I use No. 7's for flighting and No. 5's and No. 4's for jumping ducks on a river. Later on in the year I would use No. 5's and No. 4's all the time as the birds are bigger and have an extra layer of fat. On this particular occasion I took my son, Shane and his friend, Pat. Brandy, my Brittany Spaniel was going on his first 'real' shooting expedition. I wore my waders just in case we might encounter any problems when retrieving , if we were lucky to get any ducks.

It was 7.00 p.m. as we closed the doors of the jeep quietly. We were very early for the evening flight but it would be worse if somebody else came before us. The ponds average fifty yards in diameter and it would be unsafe for too many people. There were four paddocks divided by electric fencing between us and the ponds. I was delighted to see that they were devoid of cattle – many times previously I was followed by the young Friesian bull. I consider myself fairly fit but it is difficult to outrun a bull with waders on. However, I always felt safer with my shotgun in such a position than my

Old Shooting butt on the Galtees (See Chapter 1)

Brace of red grouse – September 1999 (last of the Millennium) (See Chapter 1)

Releasing Mallard into Cahir Gun Club Sanctuary (Chapter 2)

English Springer Spaniel retrieving Mallard from the flooded River Suir (Chapter 2)

Mobile Pheasant release pen (Chapter 3)

Larsen Trap with call bird to catch Magpies (Chapter 3)

Gun Club Members working hard to collect funds for charity (Chapter 3)

Fallow buck taken with a .243 Steyr-Mannlicher Rifle and a 6x42 Smith and Bender Scope
(Chapter 4)

eleven foot fly rod!

As we approached the pond paddock, four teal sprung from the open pond. We crouched down hoping that they would fly over us or land in the sheltered pond. They circled three times but then made an exit towards the Knockmealdown Mountains on the Waterford-Tipperary border. I told the two boys to stay back with Brandy as I felt that there might be more ducks in the main pond. I bent down to make my profile as low as possible and began my stalk. I could hear no 'quacks' and as yet I couldn't see anything. At the edge of the pond I peered through the bushes and saw one mallard standing on a rock and another swimming beside her. 'There must be more there!', I thought, so I slipped off the safety catch and stood on top of the embankment which concealed my approach.

The water erupted all around with startled mallard and teal. The first mallard I saw tumbled to my first shot but I missed the swimming partner. As there were ducks everywhere, I had to settle myself down for the final shot. One duck was going away directly from me and I pulled up and knocked it into the rushes. There must have been about twelve mallard or so on the pond altogether, but as they sprung from all directions, I couldn't keep an accurate count.

The two lads arrived with Brandy and he made his first real retrieve by bringing back the bird which was lying in the water. Just as I was examining the duck, three teal approached from the far side like a squadron of jet-fighters. I aimed at the lead bird, passed him out by one foot and fired. He fell in the middle of the paddock and Brandy had another excellent retrieve. It was a nice plump female bird. Ten minutes had elapsed since the first bird was shot so it was time to fetch the mallard which fell in the rushes. The Brittany searched hard but to no avail. Maybe the bird had dived and surfaced in another place or maybe it had recovered and flown away. Brandy came to point and I thought we had our mallard. I told Shane to pick up the duck but there was no sign of it. Brandy moved off point but stopped two yards further on. He was rock-steady again but neither Shane nor Pat could see any sign of the bird in the rushes. I bent down beside the dog and there was nothing visible. Suddenly Brandy moved as there was something stirring under the flattened rushes – our second mallard. Three out of three for a novice dog – not bad!

It was now 7.45 p.m. and it would be a while before the flight would begin. We placed the birds under an alder tree and positioned ourselves between the two ponds in a clump of reeds. Visibility was one hundred percent, but we could see no flocks flying or hear anyone else shooting. It was still fairly bright at 9.00 p.m. and we were getting restless after the long wait. 9.15 p.m. and we were sure that no ducks would come back. The alarm had been sent out and this was one pond not to visit tonight if you were a mallard or teal.

We got up, stretched our legs and picked up our ducks to go home. Just as I turned my back, I heard the quacking of a flock of mallard. Turning to my right, I saw a pack of seven birds which were set on landing but began to gain altitude as they saw us. I fired a left and right and the first bird fell at my feet while the other fell in the field. I had one shot left and dropped another bird in the middle of the open pond. I picked up the bird at my feet while Brandy was kept busy with the others. It was dusk now so we hid in a cluster of rushes beside the open pond.

I put on my face mask and kept my head down. The sky was full of the sound of wings whirring and ducks quacking. They had been feeding in barley fields and were coming home for the night. The crops (food bags) of the birds we had shot were full of grain. Four birds swung around to the east and began the flight in towards me. I fired just as they were forty yards out with wings outstretched and flapping backward to slow themselves down. Two birds fell into the pond twenty yards out. One of the birds was dead but the other was a winger. Brandy retrieved the dead bird first and then I sent him for the live bird. Being a young dog, I thought that he might be afraid and back away. There was no need to worry for he brought back the bird perfectly to hand. He held each bird gently and there were no tears or puncture marks in the skin.

I shot two more singles after this and missed about three more. It was approximately 9.35 p.m. and the birds were still flighting. Nine mallard and one teal was a good bag so there was no point in being greedy. We decided to leave the pond and the mallard were still flighting as we walked towards the distant sunset. If you leave a pond with duck still flighting in, you may be confident that if you visit it in a week's time there will be some there again. If an area is over-shot, the wildlife will more than likely leave for good.

Between 1993 and 1996 the N.A.R.G.C. (the National Association of Regional Game Councils) released sixteen thousand mallard into the wild. I am a member of three gun clubs which are affiliated to the N.A.R.G.C. Each club has released hundreds of mallard and set aside sanctuaries where the birds can breed. South Tipperary Regional Game Council (S.T.R.G.C.) made duck ponds at the foot of the Knockmealdowns over twenty years ago. These ponds were declared a sanctuary and duck were released there. Natural vegetation has taken hold now and the area has also been planted with conifers and deciduous trees. Wild mallard nest there and it is one of the main sources of duck for the Southern Suir Valley.

When you see mallard on rivers in towns or in parks or golf courses, you may be sure that they are there through the hard effort and money of dedicated gun club members.

CHAPTER THREE

Pheasant

Halloween, 31st October, is a special day for children and adults around the world. It is at dusk when the real celebrations begin. Children go 'trick or treating', bonfires are lit and fireworks are set off where available. At night witches are supposed to cross the face of the moon. Goblins, warlocks and all types of spirits are allowed to roam freely.

In Ireland Halloween is called Oíche Shamna or Samhain. It is a Celtic feast which has integrated with Christian traditions in more modern times. It is a feast of Thanksgiving for a good harvest, but bonfires are lit to frighten away 'púcas' or ghosts. The souls of the dead are allowed to roam freely by the God Samhain.

The Irish pheasant hunter is more concerned with November 1st – the first day of the pheasant season. The pheasant is the staple diet of the Irish shooter and the season continues to 31st January. Most pheasant hunters are members of the National Association of Regional Game Councils (N.A.R.G.C.) which promotes hunting and conservation in the Republic. A survey carried out by the organisation in 1993-1994 shows the typical mean bag per hunter is as follows:

- Cock Pheasant   5.12 per person
- Mallard   3.00 per person
- Common Snipe   3.19 per person
- Woodcock   2.46 per person
- Red Grouse   0.07 per person

The Gun Club which is generally based at parish level will have a core group of members who will have been involved in pheasant rearing and predator/vermin control during the previous year. The birds may have been bought as 6-week old poults in June or July from game farms or they may have been reared under bantam hens by the clubs own members. Suir Valley and District Gun Club is based in Clonmel, Co. Tipperary, which is one of the biggest towns in Ireland. The club reared two hundred pheasants by the use of bantam hens last year. The committee built coops and bought in bantam hens. Ten members then took two coops each and reared the birds in their own back gardens until the poults were ready to go to the release pen. Many back lawns had brown patches by the end of the summer but by the middle of autumn everything was back to its original green colour. Cahir Game Preservation Association with the assistance of the South Tipperary Regional Game Council built a mobile release pen by using 8' x 4' box metal sections. This type of pen is ideal as it can be moved to different locations each season or sometimes during the same season if the release programme was begun early. The pen can be added to or subtracted from and it is easily transported. I remember taking the pen down in fifteen minutes and erecting it again in twenty-five minutes.

There is no point in either releasing pheasants or mallard if they are going to become food for vermin like mink, magpies, grey crows and foxes. Most clubs organise fox hunts using terriers or sheepdogs during February or March. Some clubs even dispense with pheasant shooting in January in order to conserve the stock of wild birds and to concentrate on pest control. Larsen traps may be used for magpies or grey crows. An egg or a piece of fish or meat may be used to catch the call bird for the trap especially – if you wish to trap grey crows. A hen egg or a bad pheasant egg is often a good lure for the magpie. Remember that the call- bird must have adequate food and water, and that the trap should be visited regularly and trapped birds dispatched humanely.

Mink have no natural enemies in Ireland. They have escaped from mink farms where they were bred for their pelts and they now inhabit every river system in Ireland. The mink is still hunted legally in the U.S. for its pelt, and it is also hunted by the fisher which is bigger than the mink. This keeps its numbers under control but the only enemy to the mink in Ireland is the concerned gun club member. A mink which breaks into a pheasant pen will kill up to fifteen birds, yet only eat one. I have known of mink to even kill sheep and lambs. Cage traps and spring traps are used to catch mink. Near water courses a four foot section of wavin pipe can be used. One end of the pipe is set almost vertically into the ground – the bottom having been sealed with cement previously. A piece of fish or mackerel is used as bait. Great care has to be taken when removing the mink as it is a fierce adversary with razor sharp teeth.

All of this entails work and effort and of course money. Birds have to be bought, they have to be fed on various foods at different times, pens must be built, repaired and sprayed. Traps must be bought and signs must be erected around preserves and sanctuaries. I haven't even mentioned the cost of phone calls, postage, travel and all the various odds and ends which add to a gun club's expense account. Membership fees will never cover all these expenses so clay-pigeon shoots, table quizzes, duck-derbies and many other ingenius plans must be invented in order to provide adequate funds.

The pheasant (phasianidae) – an piasún as it is named in the Irish language is not native to either Ireland or the United States. Legend says that the Chinese ring necked pheasant was introduced to Europe by the Argonauts who brought it from the river Phasis. The true story is that the Romans introduced it to Europe two thousand years ago from China and the Normans introduced it to the U.K. in the 11th century. We all learned in primary school that the Normans landed in Bannow Bay, Co. Wexford in 1169 A.D. This area of Wexford is not far from where Stephen Spielberg filmed Private Ryan. The pheasant was introduced to the U.S. and Australia in the 1800's.

Pheasant habitats include; grassland, tillage, scrub, woodland, marshland and small copses. Their main diet consists of seeds, berries, grain and sugar beet. However, the pheasant is a very opportunistic bird and he will eat insects and small animals without back bones. They roost in trees at night but the hen nests on the ground. Like all game birds the pheasant will fly only short distances and then begin to glide. If a pheasant flushes from cover and flies away, you may be able to follow it if your view is not restricted.

Cock pheasants have lovely blue-green heads and necks with a large white ring. The cocks have large red flaps of skin like combs on the side of the face. The body markings may be tan, black or green with dashes of red. The long tail, which is used for balance in flight, may be up to 36" (90 cms) long. The cock may measure 75-90 cms (30-35") in total. The hens are generally smaller and of a duller appearance. They do not have the rich red flaps of the cock but they do have red skin around the eyes. Their feathers are sandy coloured with black blotches. This provides camouflage for the bird when she is incubating on the ground. She may measure 50-70 cms in length (20-28 inches). The bill of both male and female is short and strong with an off-white colour.

The cock pheasant is polygamous and in captivity the ratio is one cock per every ten hens. He is very territorial and will use his strong spurs to defend his harem. I know of one instance where a gun club member released a mature cock into an area where he thought that there was none. It was just before the breeding season and early in the morning. As the cock flew down the field a wily old resident emerged from an oak tree and proceeded to attack. To the best of my knowledge, the blow-in had to set up home in another area!

The hen lays about eleven olive-brown eggs in late May. The bird loses its scent during this period so that it cannot be detected by foxes and ground vermin. The hen pheasant is a notorious bad mother and will leave the nest entirely for even the smallest disturbance. This is one of the reasons why gun clubs release birds into the wild every year. The chicks hatch out after 21-23 days and only the mother takes care of them. They follow the female and she teaches them what to eat. They generally live in high grass or corn fields at this time and are very susceptible to chills from the rain. When there is a lot of rain in the early summer, there is a high mortality rate amongst the young birds. Another serious problem for the young birds are silage and combine harvesters. Generally farming contractors cut the crop from the outside of the field to the centre. If there are young pheasants in the field they may be rounded-up into the centre by the machines and then chopped by the blades. The best solution to this problem is to have the crop harvested from the centre towards the edges. The young birds will then escape and hide in the ditches. Some farmers leave headlands to go fallow and if there are pylons in the field, they leave a scrub area around them. This provides all wildlife with a suitable and safe habitat.

If the young pheasant poults can reach the six week old stage, they stand a good chance of survival. The cocks are beginning to take on their distinctive colouring at this stage. The birds have their full colouring by mid-October unless they were part of a late hatch or a second clutch. Gun clubs buy their pheasant poults at the six week stage from game farms and put them into release pens. As every gun club member knows, it is at this stage when all the work of feeding and watering has to be done.

The size of the release pen should depend on the number of birds which will be put in it. If birds haven't adequate space, they will peck each other and eventually birds will die. There should be sufficient cover for birds at ground level. The mobile pen is ideal as it can be moved to the most suitable area or it can be placed around trees which encourages the birds to roost out of danger. The primary wing feathers should be clipped so that the immature birds cannot escape. The birds are fed on turkey pellets first and then changed to grain. It is always best to get a bag of feed from the game farm to make the transition as smooth as possible for the poults. We often suspend a sheep's head inside the pen from a branch of a tree. When the blue-fly lays her eggs on it the maggots will fall to the ground and encourage the young birds to eat insects. The head may be hung at a lower level and this will encourage the birds to jump up for food. There will always be mortalities where pheasant rearing is concerned. A more positive attitude should be taken and we should count the numbers which survived and which hopefully will breed in the wild the following summer.

By the month of October all release pens will be empty, and the birds should be adapted to the wild. A few hens and cocks may be kept over the winter to use as breeding stock for next year. Gun licences, club membership and N.A.R.G.C. insurance should have been paid. The insurance provided by the N.A.R.G.C. compensation fund is one of the greatest assets to Irish hunters. This scheme gives basic third party and member-to-member liability protection while hunting. Personal injury, dogs being accidentally shot or poisoned, and guns accidentally broken, are covered. If a fund member's dog causes injury to livestock, to another person, or if the dog causes an accident – the fund will cover the claim. Basically, the fund provides twenty-four hour during the duration of membership.

*   *   *

I couldn't sleep on the morning of 1st November 1997. The alarm clock was set for 4.30 a.m. but my mind was full of pictures of cock pheasants flushing from beet fields. I got up at the first buzz and made the breakfast and some soup and sandwiches to sustain me during the morning. I had arranged to meet my shooting partner, Tomas, at 5.15 a.m. Just in case he might sleep it out, I was to phone him and let it ring twice – we didn't want to wake the whole family and get into trouble. My hunting gear was in the utility room, all neatly prepared since the evening before. The weather was still very 'summery' so the basic items of dress were: a light shooting vest, wellingtons, baseball cap and a belt of No. 7 and No. 5 cartridges for my twelve bore.

Outside it was mild and calm. I went to the kennel and my three year old Brittany Spaniel Bitch 'Suzie' was waiting with her ears pricked. She had seen me put the gun in the car so she knew we were going to do some serious business today. I also took the nine month old springer spaniel bitch, 'Shannon' – I would use her later on in the day if Suzie got tired.

Tomas was up when I arrived and I had a cup of coffee and toast. He had scouted the area during the last few weeks and knew where all the sugar beet and potato fields were. He had met many pheasants with 'Tug' his orange and white Brittany dog. Tug was six years old and an excellent worker both on land and in water. Tomas also worked a springer spaniel bitch called 'Jess'. Jess was very steady and stayed well to heel. If either of the Brittanys set we would get into position and Jess would be sent into the cover to flush the bird.

We got to our destination at 6 a.m. It was still dark so we remained in the car and rolled down the windows. There was no sound of any cocks crowing but the dawn was still thirty minutes away. Hunters were passing in cars pulling dog trailers. The brake lights flashed in some – maybe they had intended coming to this spot but alas it was already booked. As the first rays of sunlight shone over Slievenamon, a cock-pheasant crowed in a tree. We made a mental picture of his location and marked it for later on. Half a mile away another pheasant crowed and judging by the sound, he was flying down from his roost. The dogs could hear all this activity and you could tell that they were as excited as ourselves.

At 7 a.m. we decided to get out of the car and begin what we had been waiting for since 31st January. The dogs cleaned themselves and settled down for instructions. There was a high ditch which led into a small grove. Tomas would go down one side and I would take the other. The Brittanys would hunt the ditch but all three dogs would hunt the grove. The dogs soon picked up a scent and trailed it to the grove. We were certain that there were birds in it. Tug set on the entrance to the grove while Suzie was sniffing hard on my side. Tomas released Jess into the grove and there was a 'crow' and a flapping of wings. One cock came out forty yards in front of me and tumbled with one shot. Two other cocks broke to the far side of the grove but neither of us got a shot. We saw the direction in which they flew so we hoped to come across them later.

The next field consisted of ten acres of sugar-beet. Pheasants love beet as it provides food and cover. On this occasion the beet was dry so it made it easier to walk through. Anybody who has walked through knee high beet without waterproof leggings knows the meaning of the word 'wetting'. We decided to separate and to hunt different areas of the field. Each of us would be able to cover our own area if the dogs set in the open.

I went to the top right hand corner and immediately Suzie came to point sixty yards in front. When I was close enough I commanded her to 'push on'. A fine old rooster sprung from the beet but he flew in the direction of a farmhouse so I didn't fire. He sailed over the roof and across a road. He was safe today but maybe our paths would cross later on in the season. Suzie moved through a gap in the ditch as she was following a trail which led into a stubble-field. She set forty yards out and was rock-steady as I approached. I looked at the ground in front of her and saw a hen lying tightly in the grass between the stubble. She pushed forward and not one but two hens broke from cover. More birds for next year I hoped!

I went back to the beet field as Tomas was going down the far side. I could see that Tug was set so I stopped to view the proceedings. Tomas let the springer go forward and six pheasants flushed from the green leaves twenty yards in front of him. I saw him raise his gun but yet he didn't fire. From where I was standing I thought that at least three of the birds were cocks. I shouted across at him and asked why he let them go. Apparently they were very young birds so he decided to let them go. Tomas uses a Webley and Scott, twelve gauge side by side with one-quarter and one-half chokes. He would have had no problem in getting a right and left.

We moved down towards the end of the field and both Brittany's came to point. A cock broke to Tomas' left and he dropped it with one shot. Jess retrieved the bird gently to hand. Another big cock broke in front of me and I raised the gun to my shoulder and fired. Missed with the first! Fired the second shot – missed again! I must have been too confident after the first shot and so as a result, I must have fired too quickly. I had one shot left in my Luigi Franchi semi-automatic. It was a No. 5 cartridge and the bird was forty-five yards out. I steadied up and pulled the trigger. He tumbled but he was in a runner. Suzie looked at me in amazement but then set off to fetch him. She found him in a thick bunch of brambles after five minutes. He was an old plump bird with long spurs. He would make a nice brace for Sunday's dinner.

Our next port of call was a 'fairy-fort'. The ancient farmers in 500-1100 A.D. built round circular mounds of earth and erected wooden fences on top. In some areas there was a double or treble earthen ditch. There were huts built of daub and wattle inside the ditch with grass or reed roofs. This was the original Celtic homestead and the rath as it was called provided protection for both the family and the farm stock. There were wolves and wild boar in Ireland at this time and cattle rustling was a popular pastime. In later years, legends said that the fairies or little people built the forts. Woe and betide anybody who would damage a fairy-fort! Superstitious J.C.B. drivers would never damage such a place. Nowadays these forts are considered archaeological artefacts and are protected by law.

Five thousand years later, all that remains of these forts is the earthen rings. These have been covered in grass or shrubs. Trees grow where the fences were and provide ideal roosting areas for pheasants. The fort we approached was seventy yards in diameter and consisted of three earthen ditches. We knew that there was bound to be birds in it as it was circled by stubble fields on all sides.

We surrounded it as best we could and let the dogs loose. They picked up some hot scents and made their way towards the middle. I heard two shots from Tomas so I presumed he must have been lucky. A hen flew past my face and swung back into the trees. I heard the flapping and crowing of a cock but instead of flying out, he perched in a clump of ivy which was growing on a beech tree. Another bird was making its way through the trees so I slipped off the safety. Eventually a nice cock burst into the sky about thirty yards up. I put the gun to my shoulder, passed him out by about a foot, and fired. He fell to the ground right at my feet. One pellet had struck his head and other than that there wasn't a mark on him. The dogs came out after five minutes so I called Tomas. He had shot one bird and saw three or four hens.

We walked back to the car and had some lunch. We decided to call it a day as we had a good bag and the races were on in Clonmel that afternoon. There were plenty of birds left so we looked forward to a bountiful season.

The fairy fort is still there but we don't hunt it anymore. It is now in the middle of a Par-three, eighteen hole golf course. The pheasants are still there but they will only have problems if they don't duck their heads when they hear the word 'Four'.

CHAPTER FOUR

Fallow in the Rut

The Fallow Deer (Dama dama) or an Fia Fionn, as it is known in Irish, is a native of Mediterranean shores. Historians think that it was taken by the Normans to England and from there across the Irish Sea to Ireland. They were kept in deer parks to provide hunting and venison for the Normans who landed in Ireland in 1169 A.D. The Phoenix Park in Dublin was originally a deer park for King John and a large herd of fallow deer can be seen there to this day. Many large estates have deer parks but with migration to the cities for work and the decline of the old landlord/tenant regime, they fell into disrepair. The deer escaped and bred successfully in the wild. As a result, fallow deer are found in most mountain ranges in Ireland and also in many lowland parks. Doneraile Forest Park in County Cork has a herd of fallow deer which was introduced in 1982. In fact the first deer park in Munster was at Mallow Castle. Queen Elizabeth 1 sent two fallow bucks to the herd in 1597.

The fallow deer is smaller than the red deer but bigger than the sika. Its coat has four main varieties of colour which is more than any other deer; common (russet brown with white spots), menil, (very light brown with large white spots) ,black and albino. The first coat is typical of the summer variety. The winter coat is greyish-brown without spots.Its antlers are also different in shape to the red and sika. The Palmate or palm shaped antlers are more akin to the moose. The only other deer to have palmate antlers in Ireland was the Irish elk, also called the Giant Irish Deer. This deer has been extinct for over ten thousand years at least, but its antlers have been found in the bogs of Ireland. Some of them had a six metre span and they are often mounted over the fireplaces of banquet halls in Irish castles. Examples of Irish elk antlers can be seen in Bunratty Castle, County Clare or Cahir Castle on the banks of the River Suir in County Tipperary.

Fallow deer were considered as vermin in many forestry areas up to thirty years ago. They did a lot of damage by browsing on young trees and by thrashing the young trees with their antlers in order to remove the velvet.

People were hired to shoot the deer in order to keep them under control. There was basically no official season and all types of guns, bullets and cartridges were used.

Today however, there is a specific season for fallow which is the same for red and sika deer, that is, 1st September to 28th February for bucks; and 1st November to 31st January for does. The season for does may be lengthened if they are causing a problem due to prolific numbers. Coillte (The Irish Forestry Board) leases woodland to stalkers and part of the agreement is that they cull a certain number of deer. The lettings are put up for tender and stalkers bid privately. Sometimes a ten deer cull may go for one thousand, five hundred pounds plus V.A.T. (Value Added Tax) at twelve and a half percent per annum.

However, deer hunting may be approached from a cheaper angle. Farmers who have lands bordering forests or areas where deer live, may grant written permission to the deer hunter to enter and shoot on his or her lands. Many farmers are more than delighted to grant such, as their crops may be damaged by deer or, during the winter months, there may be only sufficient grass for the farmer's own stock. Deer often break down fences in their determination to get at good grazing. It is also a matter of debate whether the deer spread T.B. or whether they contract it from the cattle. There are also many small private plantations as a result of grants from Central Government. The land owner may lose the entitlement to get the annual grant if the trees are not properly taken care of and protected from both domestic and wild animals.

The best time to get a good fallow buck is during the rut. In some areas the rut may be earlier than in others. Weather has a lot to do with it and the majority of hunters seem to agree that cold and dry weather is necessary to bring it on. My companions and I, in our area of the South, believe that the October Bank Holiday weekend is when the rut is at its peak. When November comes the big stags seem to disappear to build up their reserves for the winter after the exertions of the mating ritual. The following story happened during the rut in 1986.

* * *

Mid October and the rut was on. The bracken had been partially burned off by the first frosts but the up-hill going was still tough. To the north, the mountains were clear and the small towns of the Golden Vale nestled amongst the fields. There was no wind and the only sound was the lonesome call of the raven in the morning air. Suddenly there was the grunt of a fallow stag a half mile to the west.

I moved quietly down to the stream at the bottom of the glen and up the two hundred foot incline through furze and briars on hands and knees. Then I heard the buck grunting two hundred and fifty yards ahead in a copse of alders. When I was within one hundred yards, he grunted again and began to move. I could see neither the buck nor the doe but he knew I was there. Finally, I reached a clearing where I could get a clear shot but all that remained was a solitary doe. The quarry was bounding noisily away in the distance – however, 'beidh lá eile ag an bPaorach'.

Eight weeks later I returned to the area. It had rained that night and the weather was mild and calm. As I closed the car door, I glanced up the valley and six hundred yards away, I saw the sun glistening on the antlers. This time I could see him but he couldn't see me. Near an abandoned farmhouse I stopped at a gate and glassed the valley. He was a big stag with five does. There was a dry wall which was parallel to the valley for two hundred yards. I crouched down behind it until I reached the open hill. The next part of the stalk was through furze, mud and bracken. All I could see were the roots of the furze in front and the blue sky overhead. When I considered that I was opposite the animal, I edged up carefully behind a large boulder. He was one hundred and fifty yards away – broadside and oblivious to my presence. His does were in a line on the mountain path behind him browsing peacefully with the odd glance around.

I crawled forward to a broken section of wall and placed the rifle on a flat mossy stone. The 6X wide angle scope displayed a fine stag standing just in front of a birch tree. Every now and then he looked up casually and continued eating the moist grass. This time the odds were in my favour. I placed the crosshairs behind his shoulder and as the shot was across a gully, I held just below the spine. A few seconds were needed to allow my breathing to slow down and the 'fever' to cool down. When the scope was steady I squeezed gently.

The report broke the stillness as the echo rumbled over the hills. With the recoil, I didn't see anything so I looked cautiously over the wall. The does were making a quick exit, crashing through the scrub yet still holding their line. The stag had tumbled down to the stream so I waited a few moments.

The animal was about five years old. He had his grey winter coat but it was very fine. He was in excellent condition but there was no fat as he must have worn himself out during the rut. The beams were thick but the palms were thin compared to the animals that roam the Phoenix Park. One of the tines was broken in half so I presumed there was another nice stag in the area.

After the gralloch, I dragged him across the stream. Then the hard work really began, I had to pull him up the one hundred and fifty feet of the glenside – twenty feet at a time – blood and sweat but no tears. Eventually I reached the brow, so it was all downhill on the slippery wet grass.

The mountains had one stag less but with some luck there would be five fawns in June. The freezer would be stocked and there would be venison for the Christening at Christmas. A black tube fly made from his tail would catch a fourteen pound Slaney salmon in the Spring.

*   *   *

The Southern Deer Society draws its membership from the provinces of Munster and Leinster in the South of the Irish Republic. The aims and objectives of the society are:
- The conservation of deer and their habitat in Ireland
- To protect the rights of legitimate deer hunters
- To record proceedings and to provide information for members
- To co-operate with other bodies in pursuance of these aims and objectives

The society organises Rifle Shoots each year; Cookery Demonstrations; Carcass Preparation Seminars; Information Nights on Wildlife and the Law; and Equipment Fairs. Art competitions are held for children, the subject being 'Wild Irish Deer'. The prize-giving consists of a lecture and then a question and answer session from the local Wildlife Ranger for the children and their parents. Various items of taxidermy are shown to the children and new electronic gadgets such as 'bat-detectors' always generate great interest. The society always has a stand at the Adare Country Fair each May. The main item of attraction is the enclosure with a fallow buck and does.

In order to carry out its aims and objectives, the Southern Deer Society set up various sub-committees which drafted up proposals for the safe and proper conduct of hunting by the members. These proposals were amended at committee meetings and finally passed at an E.G.M. The Codes and Procedures were considered so important that they are presently being studied by other hunting organisations. The Southern Deer Society has kindly allowed me to print their Codes and I think that every hunter (not only deer hunters) should study them carefully.

Southern Deer Society – Code of Conduct / Safety
- Each member is advised to get an approved gun safe
- Always treat a rifle as though it was loaded
- Each member should have knowledge of ballistics of own rifle
- Each shooting member should have third party and personal insurance or membership of N.A.R.G.C. compensation fund
- Ensure that there are no obstructions in barrel, especially when hunting in muddy or snow conditions
- A shot should never be taken if there is any risk to persons, domestic livestock or property
- No shooting one hour before dawn or one hour after sunset with artificial viewing aids
- Members should regularly check zero of scope
- Firearms laws of the State are always to be observed.

Hunting Procedure
- Proper herd management/culling to be practised for the promotion of conservation
- Always exercise constraint. Do not overshoot. Be conscious of limited game numbers
- Shots over 300 m. not to be taken due to risk of wounding or losing an animal or causing unnecessary suffering
- If a wounded animal cannot be found, the help of a dog handler should be sought
- Offal should be disposed of correctly
- Target must be properly identified, i.e. pricket/doe.

Strict Code of Conduct
- No counting of deer by lamp at any time, unless Wildlife Ranger and local Gardaí are informed
- Members are to abide by landowners wishes at all times
- Do not worry livestock or damage fences, etc.
- Be aware of the noise factor and have due regard for others in their leisure activities, and do not shoot near dwellings or farmsteads
- Any member caught trespassing with a rifle on lands where he/she has not got authorisation to hunt or breaking the above code of conduct will after giving evidence to the committee and following a fair and impartial hearing, be subject to the decision of the committee.

Guidelines for Disciplinary Action may be as follows:
- Shall be reprimanded
- Suspended
- Banned from the Society

Lettings
- Proper notification to be given to Forester – 48 hours
- All entrances to be sign-posted and nails removed when signs are taken down
- Shooting to stop at MIDDAY.

General
- Members are requested to be available to extinguish fires which threaten State Forests
- The management of the Society shall be the function of the committees. As deer stalking is not considered a professional sport, each member is requested not to shoot quarry for commercial gain. Profiteering will do nothing positive for the image of our sport.

Páirceanna Náisiúnta agus An Fiadhúlra      *National Parks and Wildlife*

NATIONAL PARKS AND WILDLIFE

WILDLIFE ACT, 1976 - SECTION 29

LICENCE TO HUNT EXEMPTED WILD MAMMALS

Licence Number DL

The Minister for Arts, Heritage, Gaeltacht and the Islands in exercise of the powers vested in her by Section 9 and 29 of the Wildlife Act, 1976 hereby grants to:

JOHN LALOR

a licence authorising him/her to hunt and kill deer with firearms (subject to the restrictions contained in section 33 of the said Act) pursuant to and in accordance with such order (if any) made under Section 25 of the said Act as is for the time being in force.

This licence shall remain in force for the period beginning on the date hereof and ending on the next 31st day of July and the authority conferred by the licence shall be exercisable for such period as is specified in the said Order (if any) made under section 25 of the Act.

Dated this 3rd day of September 1999

For the Minister for Arts, Heritage, Gaeltacht and the Islands.

Bernard Moloney
....
An officer authorised in that behalf by the said Minister.

John Lalor
....
Signature of Holder.

--- NOTE ---

Nothing in this licence authorises the holder to enter onto any lands or to hunt thereon without the permission of the owner

NATIONAL PARKS & WILDLIFE SERVICE

1999/2000 HUNTING SEASONS FOR WILD BIRDS AND WILD MAMMALS

SPECIES	OPEN SEASON
Red Grouse	1 September to 30 September
Mallard, Teal, Gadwall, Wigeon, Pintail, Shoveler, Scaup, Tufted Duck, Pochard, Goldeneye, Golden Plover, Snipe, Jack Snipe.	1 September to 31 January
Red-Legged Partridge	1 November to 31 January
Cock Pheasant Woodcock	1 November to 31 January
Curlew	1 November to 30 November
Canada Geese *(Countrywide)* Canada Geese *(Co. Cavan and Co. Leitrim only)* and excluding the following townlands: Eonish Island, Rinn and Deramfield (Cavan) and the River Shannon (Leitrim)	1 Sept. to 30 Sept. 1 October to 31 January
Greylag Geese *(Countrywide)* Greylag Geese *(Lady's Island, Co. Wexford and Gearagh East Gearagh West in Co. Cork only).*	1 Sept. to 30 Sept. 1 October to 31 January
Woodpigeon	1 June to 31 January

SPECIES		COUNTIES		
Deer		Dublin & Wicklow	Kerry	All Other Counties
Red	Male	1 September to 28 February	No Season	1 September to 28 February
	Female	1 November to 28 February	No Season	1 November to 31 January
Sika	Male	1 September to 28 February	1 September to 28 February	1 September to 28 February
	Female	1 November to 28 February	1 November to 31 January	1 November to 31 January
Fallow	Male	1 September to 28 February	1 September to 28 February	1 September to 28 February
	Female	1 November to 31 January	1 November to 31 January	1 November to 31 January

SPECIES	OPEN SEASON
Hares (excluding the following townlands in Co. Wexford: North East Slob, North West Slob, Big Island, Beggerin Island and the Raven.	26 September to 28 February

CHAPTER FIVE

Crop Protection
– Pigeons and Crows

We hunt and shoot in Ireland because of the generosity of the farming community. Farmers allow sportsmen to enter their lands in the pursuit of game and in ninety-five percent of cases they do not levy a charge. The N.A.R.G.C. and the I.F.A. (Irish Farmers Association) are closely linked. Many farmers are also members of rural gun clubs. In order to repay the farmer for his or her gratitude, we have to be prepared to help with vermin control and crop protection.

Crop protection generally takes place during the months of July and August. Corn and pea crops are the main items which need protection during this time. This present summer (1999) has been very dry and there has been little or no wind. The barley crops are ripening and in some cases winter barley has been harvested already. Barley and wheat crops take on a golden colour when they are ripening. The main test however is to get a head of corn, rub the grains between your hands, and blow away the chaff. Now place a grain or two between your teeth and bite down. If it is hard to crush it is ripe, but if it is soft and moist, it needs more time. Barley is a very important cash crop for farmers and it is also important for the economy of the country. Barley is brewed to make Guinness in St. James' Gate in Dublin, and distilled to make Bushmills whiskey in County Antrim, in the North of Ireland.

The summer of 1997 was one of the wettest in recent times. Not alone was it wet but it was also extremely stormy. Rain causes corn crops to become heavy and if a strong wind comes, the stalks are easily knocked. Once a small area or pocket of corn has been flattened, it begins to enlarge with every windy day. Birds such as pigeons and crows are able to fly in and they knock and eat more with each day. A small flock of ten or fifteen birds may make the initial attack but the word seems to spread and soon there may be hundreds of birds feasting to their hearts contents.

Farmers sometimes use crow-bangers. This is a type of gas-tube which makes a bang like a shot gun at certain intervals. Occasionally, a farmer puts a scarecrow in the field or a silhouette of a man – sometimes even one which seems to be carrying a gun. The most modern method is a helium filled balloon which is tethered over the crop in question and suspended from this may be an outline of a hawk. Apparently this frightens the birds as they feel uneasy if a 'bird of prey' is hovering above them. I have been told that this particular item can cost up to two hundred pounds.

All of the above methods are costly. Individual shooters and gun clubs should always be prepared to help the farmer in these circumstances. Some gun clubs may even advertise their services in the local papers, and in many other cases, the farmer makes direct contact with the hunters who he is personally acquainted with. The shooter is providing a needy service to the land owner but it may also be an exhilarating day's sport.

The casual pigeon or crow shooter will go out to the corn field and lie in wait near a ditch which is under the flight line. Alternatively he or she may conceal themselves in the corn but in range of where the birds are landing. A game gun with half and full chokes is quite adequate. The cartridges to use are No. 7½'s or No. 8's.

The more professional pigeon controller will wear camouflage clothing and even a face mask. Equipment will include netting, posts and decoys. A cooler with an ample supply of food and soft drinks is also important. The weather may be sultry and balmy and if the shooting is good, people may stay all day in the field.

Decoys may be laid out in a 'V' position facing into the wind. A couple of individual birds may be set out to the side. When shooting in fields of peas, I put some of the decoys on top of the plants. You should place the decoys in the lodged corn when you are shooting in barley or wheat fields. Dead birds can be added to the decoys. Sometimes a forked twig is placed under the bird's head to hold it in position. A 'flapper' is a great way of attracting birds. It may consist of a dead bird fixed to a springing frame while the wings are kept out- stretched. The 'flapping' or flying motion of the wings is a great attraction to other pigeons. A cheaper method of making a 'flapper' is to get a sally or willow rod, push it through the rectum and up to the bird's beak, but not out through it. Next get a piece of wire which is strong enough to go through one wing, through the chest cavity and out through the other wing. The suppleness of the willow rod and wire will cause the bird to move gently in the wind. Some hunters mark off an area of lodged wheat with construction tape. This will deter the birds from landing and entice them to the area which has been decoyed. Pigeons can also be shot when they are returning to their roosting areas. Windy weather is always best and some great sporting shots may be had.

The N.A.R.G.C. has requested that members keep the wings of pigeons as part of their pest control program. Many people remove the breast meat from the pigeons as the dark flesh has a lovely flavour. Game dealers reputedly were paying up to twenty pence for a pigeon at one stage. Rumour had it that some restaurants were charging seventeen pounds for pigeon on the menu! Crows may be hunted in similar fashion to pigeons but they are not as wiley or fast, and I do not know anybody who eats crows.

My fellow hunters tell me that pigeons are scarce at the moment, yet I know some people who have shot over two hundred and three hundred birds recently in two consecutive days. The pigeon is a game species now under European Union law with its own particular season. Pigeons may breed up to three times a year but due to the interest in this aspect of shooting, hunters are beginning to worry if the pigeon has a proper opportunity to breed adequately.

The Passenger Pigeon in North America numbered countless millions during the last century. They were considered pests and a bounty was put on them. They were shot but this did not control their numbers. Then they were netted in the trees where they used nest in huge numbers. They were also poisoned. This didn't really dent the numbers until it was decided to dynamite the birds. When the birds went to roost, they were dynamited in their thousands. Apparently the Passenger Pigeons needed a large population to keep its breeding capabilities viable. The numbers fell to such a low level that the birds weren't able to breed in sufficient numbers. Gradually their numbers dwindled and they are now extinct. The last one died in the Bronx Zoo in 1901. There will never be a Passenger Pigeon again. Hopefully our pigeon, an colúr as he is known in Irish, will be heard cooing in the ivy trees in the coming Millennium.

CHAPTER SIX

Ferrets and Ferreting

The ferret is a member of the weasel family, mustelidae. It is a small mammal which is an ancestor of the European polecat which was domesticated by man over time. In Ireland the black and white ferret is also called a polecat. The polecat is mainly black and white or brown in colour. The white or albino ferret with its pink eyes is slightly smaller than the polecat. The albino is often nicknamed the 'greyhound'. Weasels are not present in Ireland but stoats are. A ferret is roughly about two to three times as large as a stoat. If you hold a ferret in your hands, you will feel how agile, slender and muscular its body is.

The ferret is a relentless hunter and its main diet consists of rodents and especially rabbits. It needs raw meat which supplies it with iron, but it also thrives on a diet of bread and milk. Indeed it is because of its love for rodents that the ferret became so popular amongst the rural community. Many people who own ferrets feed them on crows and the offal of animals such as the lungs of a deer.

Their habitat originally consisted of banks and burrows. Ferrets kept in captivity must have proper accommodation which should be spacious, with two compartments, one for sleeping and one for exercise. The hutch should be well aerated but in a sheltered place. The roof of the hutch should be sloping and waterproof. The sleeping compartment could be two feet square and about eighteen inches high. The exercise room could be three feet to one metre square. The hutch should be cleaned out regularly as the ferrets are susceptible to mange, fleas and distemper. A well cared-for ferret will hunt better than an ill-treated one.

The male ferret is called a buck or hob, the female a doe or jill. The young are referred to as kits. Ferrets, like all animals, should be bred from good stock only. The hobs should not be allowed too many jills. Jills may die if they are not mated in season. During gestation the doe should be well fed. There should be milk and water available to her at all times. The kits are born after seven weeks and there may be from five to nine in the litter. The family should have ample privacy during the first few weeks, but then the kits should be fed about three times a day.

From six weeks onwards, the kits should be handled regularly to prepare them for hunting. If you wish to pick up a young ferret, do so without hesitation, but do not change your mind and pull back your hand swiftly. The ferret has a natural inclination to strike and bite something which acts in such a manner. Ferrets which are used to being handled will become quite friendly. Ferrets are kept in Ireland for hunting purposes but I saw a pet ferret in Boston being taken for a walk on a lead and harness through a public park!

Training a ferret to hunt can commence at nine or ten weeks. A dead rabbit or rat is a useful item at this stage. Hold the rabbit in front of their noses and when they grab it, pull it away immediately. The youngsters will be disappointed but they will learn to seize and hold on the next time. The ferret is a very intelligent animal and takes to training like a pup. If they are given a particular 'call' word, they will follow their master like a litter of puppies. An area with a single rabbit hole should be fenced off and the young kits could hunt it with their mother. Alternatively a dead rabbit may be placed near a bolt hole with a string attached. The rabbit can be pulled away slowly and the kits will have great fun tugging at the 'live' prey. Young ferrets should not be trained on live rats as these can be more than a match for even a mature ferret. The young ferrets should not be muzzled at this stage until they are more mature and being put to ground.

Ferrets were originally used for controlling rabbits that were damaging crops. There was a poultry shop in my local town which up to fifteen years ago had a good supply of fresh rabbits during the winter. The rabbit killed by a ferret was basically unmarked compared to those that might have been shot by a twelve gauge shotgun or a .22 LR. I know of no place, barring Dubin, where you can get fresh wild rabbit today. There are still a few dedicated ferreting-people in South Tipperary but nowadays it is carried out for sport and for private consumption. Indeed ferret racing seems to be a popular pastime at the moment. Apparently three to four ferrets 'race' each other through 6 cm diameter transparent pipes. Each ferret is designated its own tube and a slide is pulled to release the 'horses'. First past the post is declared the winner.

Ferrets are transported in boxes with separate compartments. There are generally two compartments made of wood and with a strong wire mesh section in the front. This ensures that the ferrets travel in a comfortable well-aerated environment, and are in a healthy condition to begin hunting. A ferret may be muzzled when put to ground and he may also have a bell as a locator. The more modern way is to use electronic locators which are battery operated. They are worked on the same principle as the tracking collars used on hounds but they have a much smaller range as the animal is underground.

The ferret should be given a drink before it commences hunting and the muzzle should be checked to see that it is not too tight. The hunting location should be approached quietly and work a hedge upwind. Dogs should be kept under control – no running about or barking. One method of trapping the rabbits is to put purse-nets over the holes. The purse net looks similar to a large hair net or an old string purse. It is about two feet long and eight inches wide. When the rabbit bolts into the net, it closes at the front because his weight and momentum are pulling forward. The purse net is generally anchored to the ground by a wooden peg. Sometimes the ferret may kill the rabbit in the burrow and then lie up or sleep there. The ferret will then have to be located and dug out. If the ferret is put on a collar and line, it may be pulled out in such circumstances. The line could have knots tied every three feet or metre; the rabbiter can then judge the depth of the ferret and dig him out. A small iron-bar is often used to find the underground tunnels. If the bar meets a tunnel it will fall through quickly. These bars are generally about four feet long with a handle on top.

Another method for trapping the rabbit once it has been bolted by the ferret is to use field nets. The field net is generally ten feet to three metres in length, and about three feet to one metre high. Wooden stakes about four feet high and about one metre apart are used to keep it in position. Hazel plants may be used as the stakes or any piece of wood which is about one and a half to two inches in diameter. The field nets like the purse nets are made out of cotton or natural material. The meshes should be small enough to stop the rabbit from breaking through. The rabbit may be caught by the terriers or by the persons themselves. The number of field nets will depend on the size and the terrain of the area being hunted.

The muzzles should be checked during the day to make sure that they are not too tight. The ferrets should be given a drink of milk half way through the hunting day. Ferrets cost between five and fifteen pounds. Ferrets have a life span of five to six years.

The hunting season generally takes place between October and Christmas depending on the amount of rabbits available. Rabbits are very plentiful in some areas of Ireland, particularly in the South, but in the West they are scarce. Some ferreters say that their scarcity is due to myxomatosis – a contagious disease of rabbits. Others say that it is the fear of this disease which has caused the decline in the consumption of wild rabbits.

CHAPTER SEVEN

Driven Pheasants

The majority of pheasant hunters in Ireland go rough shooting. This means that they generally hunt in pairs using one or two dogs. The pheasants which they pursue come from the native wild stock or they may have been released by the local gun club. The general number of birds shot may be two or three pheasants per day – more birds are shot in the earlier part of the season and numbers dwindle towards the end of January. Many gun clubs stop shooting pheasants after New Year's Day to allow birds to prepare for the breeding season.

Driven shoots are practised a lot in the U.K. There may be driven shoots for red-grouse in the Highlands of Scotland or driven pheasant shoots which take place throughout England, Scotland, Wales and Northern Ireland. Driven pheasant shoots are now becoming very popular in the Republic of Ireland. Driven partridge shooting is quite common in England and it is also growing in popularity in Ireland.

Driven pheasant shooting may be organised by hotels, large estates and private individuals or companies who lease farming lands or forestry. This type of shooting is an enterprise and as such it hopes to make a good return while providing a service for which there is an ever-increasing demand. Good shoots which provide large numbers of birds can demand high fees for a day's shooting. The costs of a day's sport may range from two hundred and fifty pounds to over one thousand pounds per day. However the number of birds may vary from one hundred to six hundred and fifty birds per day. At one time the shooter paid a lump sum and then paid so much per bird which he or she shot. Nowadays the trend seems to be for an overall price regardless of the number of birds which are shot. Needless to say, shoots which command high prices always provide quality pheasants in good numbers. Cowboy operators will not last long as the word will spread if people realise that they are being conned.

The rough-shooter pursues a pheasant which on the law of averages flies away from him. The hunter who goes driven-shooting remains in a certain place and the birds fly to and over him. The birds are 'driven' by beaters and people using dogs to flush the birds from cover. Springer spaniels are the favourite dog for driven-shoots but they must be well disciplined and work in line and with the group. The beaters are generally controlled by the head-keeper who begins the hunt with a blow from a horn or whistle and signals the end of shooting in the same manner. The shooter doesn't necessarily need a dog as there will also be 'pickers-up' present to retrieve dead or injured birds. The pickers-up generally use black labradors or golden retrievers. Some shooters use their own dogs to retrieve downed birds but the important thing to remember is that the dog must be very steady and work well to the whistle.

There are on average ten guns at a driven pheasant shoot and each gun picks his peg by drawing a number. When the shooter has shot at a particular stand on the first drive, he advances two numbers on the following drive. I know of one particular driven shoot where the host takes the guests to the local hostelry. Here the guests are given a glass of sherry. Underneath the base of each glass, there is a number which corresponds to a particular peg on the first drive.

The rules of the particular shoot are explained to all participants. Any infringement of the rules is taken seriously and the offender may even be asked to leave the shoot if the organiser believes it to be a serious offence. Ground game is not shot and birds are generally taken above the tops of the trees. Firing across or down the line of the other guns is frowned upon.

The original shotguns for driven shooting were twelve bore game guns with one-quarter to three-quarters choke. They were side by sides and were made in matched pairs. The shooter had a loader who emptied and loaded his gun after every shot. Birds may be taken behind on some drives. A pair of matched shotguns bearing an English brand-name could cost anything from twelve thousand pounds to twenty thousand pounds. A normal game gun or sporting gun is quite adequate for driven pheasants today. I have never seen a 'loader' at any of the shoots which I attended. Semi-automatics are never allowed at driven shoots. Most people use side-by-sides or under and overs. When the shooters are moving to the different drives, the guns are unloaded and carried in shoulder sleeves. Both cock and hen pheasants may be shot at driven shoots. The shoots basically follow the same season as that stipulated by the states game laws but they generally are allowed an extension to the season. A particular drive on a driven shoot may be shot on average only one day in every two weeks.

I have attended driven pheasant shoots both as a shooter and as a driver or beater using English springer spaniels. In January of 1997 I was invited to shoot at the Shelton shoot which is beside Shelton Abbey in County Wicklow. Peter Butler and I were asked to share a gun for the day and our hosts were Michael and Betty Phelan. There was a chance of snow so we travelled to Dublin the previous day from Tipperary. Michael and Betty provided us with comfortable lodgings in their house which was about forty miles from the shoot. Dinner that evening consisted of fine wine and turkey. The turkey was not from the local supermarket but from Michael's shoot in Wicklow. The meat was very tender and much more moist when compared to the commercial variety. If we were lucky we might shoot one of them the following day.

We had breakfast at 6.30 a.m. and soon we were driving through the Wicklow Mountains. The weather was mild with a slight breeze so the chances of a snow-storm had vanished. White puffs of clouds sailed over the Sugarloaf Mountain as the rising sun caused the loose quartz on the summit to glisten like snow. At 8.30 a.m. we were driving into the shoot's headquarters.

The Shelton Shoot is not a commercial driven shoot but a club consisting of 10 'guns'. Each member or 'gun' may own a 'full' or 'half-gun'. The members fund the rearing of birds and pay for the services of a game keeper. The Club holds an A.G.M. and elects a 'Captain', Chairperson and Secretary/Treasurer to administrate the shoot. The Captain is in charge of proceedings on the actual shooting days. Guests may be invited and the odd-day may be sold to defray costs. Membership of the shoot may be opened if a vacancy arises.

Here we were introduced to the other nine members of the shooting party. Everybody had a mug of tea or coffee which helped to warm us. Procedures and safety rules were explained, pegs numbers were drawn and we all walked quietly to the first drive. Peter told me to shoot in the first drive as he had shot here on numerous occasions in the past. He would stand behind me and load the gun. I was using a Webley and Scott, twelve gauge ejector with half and three-quarter chokes. The barrels were twenty-eight inches long and I loaded No. 7 shot in each barrel.

I was quite nervous as I did not want to make any mistakes. We were standing on a forest road with twenty to thirty foot high pine trees on either side. The birds should be shot above the trees in front as they appeared and about thirty yards to my right and left. The beaters could be heard making their ways through the undergrowth and the odd pheasant was running ahead of them. A pure white bird ran for fifty yards through the trees in front of me but then flew to a perch about fifteen feet from the ground and remained there right throughout that particular drive. Suddenly a flock of about twelve birds crossed three pegs down to my right and a number of shots rang out. I saw one bird fall in the trees behind and another on the side of the road. The beaters were working from my right and soon most of the guns below me were firing. I prepared to fire as the sound of the beaters approached. A hen came over high to my left but I didn't shoot as I thought it was nearer to the peg on my left. Suddenly the whistle blew and the first drive was over. I hadn't fired a shot but I certainly had learned a lot.

It was Peter's turn to shoot on the next drive, so I stood behind him. The drive was from left to right and Peter was on the last peg on that drive. He had fifty to sixty years of shooting experience and was recognised as a good shot with both a shotgun and rifle. The whistle sounded to start the drive so we both waited eagerly. Shots rang out further up the line and the birds must have been very plentiful as the sounds followed in rapid succession. A pheasant appeared two hundred yards to our right, moving swiftly as it glided down the hill between the trees. One shot rang out and it tumbled to the ground in a puff of feathers. Two more birds appeared and met the same fate. The shooters up the line were good shots and not one bird made it as far as Peter's peg. We were not in the least disappointed as it was a pleasure to watch experienced, careful gunmen in the pursuit of their sport.

The keeper blew the whistle again and so the second drive came to an end. A rough-shooter is constantly on the move and for that reason he or she remains warm. I wasn't wearing a shooting jacket as the morning appeared quite mild. My shooting vest was very light so I was now beginning to feel cold. We all gathered together and one of the guests produced a thermos-flask with hot 'mulled-wine'. Mulled-wine keeps the skiers warm on the Austrian Alps and it certainly helped me stay warm in the foothills of the Wicklow Mountains.

I was to shoot in the next drive and I had progressed to a peg which was near the centre. Again the drive was between sections of the pine forest and Peter and I were standing as far back on the road as we could in order to get ample time to swing and aim at the birds. We were facing east and the sun was shining with just a few clouds in the sky. It was a perfect setting to single out a fast flying pheasant. Some of the pheasants were of a small Swedish breed which gave them great powers of acceleration. Many of the birds were travelling in excess of sixty miles per hour when in full flight.

The whistle blew so we knew that the drive was about to begin. Almost simultaneously, a lone hen appeared about fifteen feet above the tree tops. I mounted the Wembley and Scott to my right shoulder, followed her line of flight, passed her out and pulled the trigger. A puff of feathers proved that I was on target and a thump twenty feet behind marked the spot for the picker-up. A cock crowing from the top of the hill behind the trees warned me that a large group of pheasants was approaching. Sure enough a flock of twenty to thirty birds appeared and I had a left and right. As the empty cartridges ejected, Peter popped in two more and I was back in action again. The other guns were also seeing plenty of birds and it proved to be the best drive of the day so far. The whistle sounded which gave the barrels of the guns a chance to cool down.

I had marked one cock pheasant which had fallen in a drain beside the forest road. There was one clump of grass there and the bird had hidden underneath it. The only thing which gave the bird's presence away was the long protruding tail. A glossy coated black labrador scented the bird, picked it up gently and soon it was back at the collection point.

It was 12.30 p.m. and time to adjourn for lunch. We followed the cavalcade of jeeps and cars through forest roads, passed by a golf course where the Avoca river[Thomas Moore wrote about the Vale of Avoca in his poem 'The Meeting of the Waters'] meandered by and soon we were in front of the Woodenbridge Hotel which was nestled deep in the mountains. The weather had turned cool and misty, but the hotel was warm, cheery and bustling with people. The main course consisted of either beef, lamb or turkey. Everybody ate heartily and quenched their thirsts with fine claret and white wine. More introductions were made as the guests' partners had joined them for the meal. Many 'tall' tales were told and red faces were hidden by the heat of the dining room.

Peter took the peg for the first drive after lunch. He was also using a Webley and Scott game gun. He downed the first few birds with single shots and I was kept busy popping the two cartridges into the breech for him each time. Peter had the Webley for over fifteen years and the recoil pad was well worn from use. The odd scratch on the stock may have come from a fall on the Knockmealdowns when hunting grouse or from climbing over whitethorn ditches in the valley of the Suir when hunting pheasants or mallard.

The light was fading fast as the last drive of the day approached. It was situated at the side of a hill which was covered in deciduous trees and with a thick layer of brambles or blackberry bushes on the forest floor. The birds would be driven from the top of the hill and they would fly downwards to open countryside which consisted of fields covered in bracken and furze which were skirted by the small river which I mentioned earlier. The wood wasn't as dense as the earlier pine forests so there was a good chance of getting a shot at the birds as they swerved and glided between the oaks and birches.

It was Peter's turn to shoot but he insisted that I take his place. After friendly argument, it was agreed that I would shoot for the first half of the drive and that we would share the remainder. At this stage of the day I felt confident and it showed in my shooting. A fine cock crew before taking off from the hilltop. I noticed his s-shaped flight path through the trees and as he passed in front I fired. He fell about ten feet in front of me into a clump of brambles. The birds were very plentiful on this drive so after I had half a dozen in the bag I passed the gun to Peter. He shot extremely well and not one bird passed our peg. The guns up and down the line were having some great action also. Twelve thousand birds and more are reared on this shoot and we were reaping the rewards of all the hard work which had been carried out by the keeper and his assistants over the previous spring and summer. The mist was now changing to drizzle and rain when the whistle sounded to bring a conclusion to a most enjoyable day.

We returned to the meeting point where the birds which had been picked up were tied together to form braces, that is, one cock and one hen. All the birds were in perfect condition due to the way they had been reared. The dogs which were used certainly had soft mouths as was evidenced by the untorn skins on the pheasants. Each shooter was given a brace of birds. It was almost the last shoot of the season and the final tally between the nine guns was two hundred and thirty-five. This was a great result when you consider that there were many six hundred and fifty bird days which had taken place previously.

Peter and I thanked our hosts and began the long drive back to Tipperary. The following Sunday my family had roast pheasant for dinner. The fat on their breasts made them all the tastier and even though we didn't have turkey on the plate, they were as good as last year's Christmas dinner.

As I write this chapter, the law with regard to tourist shooters in Ireland is being revised. The promoters of many shoots suffered this year as some foreign clients were unable to attend due to problems with licensing. Driven pheasant shoots do not affect the native pheasant population. It is a 'put and take' enterprise and it actually adds to the local population of birds. The birds which leave the shoot increase the numbers of the native population and some of the birds from the shoot breed in the wild. Shoot organisers keep vermin under control all year round. Many of the mature birds are trapped when the season is over and sold to gun clubs. I know of instances where commercial shoot organisers have given birds free to local clubs to help increase pheasant numbers in the wild and to promote good relations. Hopefully this co-operation will last into the new Millennium for the good of all wildlife in Ireland.

CHAPTER EIGHT

Fox Hunting

An Maidrín Rua, Rua, Rua,
An Maidrín Rua at· gr·nna;
An Maidrín Rua ina luÌ sa luachair,
Is barra dhá chluas in airde.

This is a verse of an Irish song which is learned by many Irish children in Elementary School. It describes the red fox; an maidrín rua; the little red dog. The fox is described as a nasty little creature; he is hiding in the rushes and the tips of his ears are protruding above them.

American hunters say that if there is a Third World War and the earth is destroyed, there will be only two species which will survive: the cockroach and the coyote. If Ireland is devastated by such an event I am sure that the red fox will survive. We have all heard the similes 'As sly as a fox'; 'As cunning as a fox'; and 'As cute as a fox'. Anybody who has had any dealings with foxes or studied their characteristics, will know that these comparisons are very suitable.

The male fox is called a dog; the female a vixen; and the young a cub. The coat is generally a reddish or rusty brown, and the underparts are white. The ears are very triangular in shape and the outside tips are a matte black. The muzzle is thin and tapers to a point which is ideal for catching small rodents in the grass. The legs are slender and the fox may measure up to 36 cms (18 ins) at the shoulder.

The tail is the object which most of us associate with the fox and is almost always referred to as the 'Brush'. The tail is bushy and it keeps the fox balanced when it pounces on its prey. The tail may be 18 cms to 40 cms in length. It is rusty brown and may have a white tip at the end in the case of the dog fox. The tips of the red hairs may be black on some brushes. There is a scent gland on the upper part of the brush and the tail is used to spread the strong musty smell which even the human nose can detect.

The red fox can be found everywhere in Ireland. They are generally associated with woodland, small copses and dense undergrowth such as furze bushes. They can also be found on the bare mountain tops far above the tree line. With the increase in urbanisation, foxes have moved into towns and cities. I know of one case where a vixen built her earth under a prefabricated building which was being used as a classroom. A nasty smell began to build up in the room and on inspection, the vixen was found with a litter of cubs. Glad to say that the family was reared before the vixen moved on to different pastures. The fox was introduced to Australia by the English for hunting purposes and it survives well in many hot desert type areas. The habitat beyond the Arctic Circle does not seem to be able to support the red fox but its cousin, the Arctic fox survives well in such an environment. Foxes belong to the family canidae. The European red fox belongs to the genus and species Vulpes Fulva; the North American red fox is Vulpes Vulpes; the Arctic fox is Alopex Lagopus and the grey fox is Vulpes Cinereoargenteus.

The red fox is a predator and a carnivore. It would be better however to term him an omnivore as he is an opportunist where food is concerned. Foxes feed on lambs, fowl, pheasants, rabbits, mice, rats and voles to name but a few items on the menu. They will also eat carrion and they will often search public highways in search of road kills. A fox may take just one chicken in a coop or one pheasant from a release pen, but he will kill and injure many more in the process. Rural foxes enter the urban environment by following railway tracks and canal banks. They seem to steer clear of houses where the pet dog is on the loose but if the fox is not disturbed, he will raid rubbish bins and also large refuse dumps.

Foxes mate in late January and early February. The vixen calls in a high pitched scream and the dog answers in a series of barks or short howls. A frosty, star lit night is an ideal time to hear their love songs. Gestation takes fifty-three days (the household dog gestates for sixty-three days) and four cubs are generally born – litters as high as twelve have been documented in some areas. The den or earth is generally a large burrow by a ditch, in a quarry or in small wood or copse. Both parents have to hunt to feed the cubs once they have been weaned. They leave the family unit in the autumn to find a territory of their own. Red foxes reach sexual maturity at eight to nine months. Foxes are very territorial and mark their areas with faeces and scent. The dog fox guards his territory but he may allow an overlap with a number of females.

Gun clubs have fox drives or shoots when the pheasant season closes. Pheasants will be released on club preserves; mature birds during the spring and poults during the summer. Foxes have to be culled if the birds are to have a chance to mate and breed. The method of hunting with guns is to surround a culvert with guns; hunt or drive it with terriers or in some cases spaniels; when the fox breaks from cover he is shot. The guns at the starting point must always be on the alert as many wily foxes backtrack when the dogs and beaters have gone past. It is best to hunt into the wind but due to the location of the cover, this may not be possible. The area to be hunted should be approached quietly as foxes like to lie out in the early spring sunshine and they will hear or see a noisy shooting party and exit the area before it has been sealed off. Gun clubs rely on the goodwill of the farmers and controlling foxes is one way of showing appreciation.

The term 'fox hunting' to the majority of people in Ireland, the U.K. and North America means hunting the red fox using purpose bred hounds while mounted on horseback. Foxhunting amongst the hunting fraternity is better known as 'riding to hounds'. It originated in England in the 1700's and was spread to Ireland, the U.S., New Zealand and Australia by the landlords and colonists. The riders are called the 'field' and the person in charge of the hounds is called the 'huntsman'. The 'master of foxhounds' is the person in charge of the entire organisation of the hunt. Many famous people have followed the hunt including George Washington who assembled a pack of his own in 1767 in Mount Vernon. Washington's wife, Martha, used also accompany him and Thomas Jefferson was an eager follower also. Mr. Charles J. Haughey who was a former Taoiseach of Ireland, was a keen follower of hounds. There are many famous packs of hounds in Ireland including the Galway Blazers, the Scarteen (The Black and Tans) and of course the Tipperary Foxhounds.

Another section of Ireland's venery or hunting heritage is the Trencher-fed packs. They are the simplest and most modest exposition of hunting with a pack of hounds. The hounds are not kept in a central kennel but at home with their individual owners. They meet at an appointed place, join together for their day's sport, and then go home their separate ways. Hunts generally take place on Sundays and they are based in both city and rural areas. The Cork Southern Harriers is one notable pack as well as the famous Kerry packs such as the Ballinskelligs, Valentia and the Glen. There are approximately five hundred foot-packs or trencher-fed packs in Ireland. Trencher-fed packs generally consist of beagles or harriers. Beagles are close in build to foxhounds, but smaller. Harriers have a heavier head than a foxhound, and may be blue mottled in colour.

Foxhounds have a coarse coat and are taller than beagles and harriers. They are bred for their superior scenting powers. The pack is kept in one central kennel and they are also bred to suit the terrain in which they hunt. They may be black and tan in colour, the Tipperary Foxhounds are tan, white and blue in colour – it would be easier to describe them as being multicoloured.

Beagles hunt hares – harriers hunt hare or fox or both. Beagles are 16" or less, Harriers are 20" hounds, the most famous of which are the Kerry Beagles – the only mounted pack being the Scarteens (Black and Tan). There are a number of these breeds of harriers. Colouring can range from white to tricolour to blue mottled. Foxhounds can range up to 25" to 26". The rough coated are Welsh or Fell hounds. Foxhounds do not necessarily have greater scenting powers than Harriers or Beagles, rather the reverse.

The fox-hunting season begins in October and ends in early March. The season coincides with the particular time when least disruption can be caused to farmlands and to stock. Cubbing or hunting the young foxes takes place from mid-August to October. I do not ride to hounds myself but each year my family and I and many of our friends attend the opening meet of the Tipperary foxhounds which takes place on the Bank Holiday Monday in October.

The present (1999) masters of the Tipperary foxhounds are Mr. Tim Hyde, Mr. Paul Ronan and Mr. Jack Ronan. The huntsman is Simon Probin and the whipper-in is Pat O'Brien. There are forty-five couple of hounds which are kennelled in Tullamaine, Fethard, and the hounds are the property of the committee. The hunt meets on Mondays, Wednesdays, Thursdays and Saturdays at 11 a.m. The country is in County Tipperary and the best centres are Fethard, Cashel, Cahir, Gooldscross and Clonmel. The hunt is over one hundred and seventy-five years old. The kennels were kept by the Barton family in Grove which is outside Fethard, but they were moved to Tullamaine in 1919. Tullamaine, or Tulach Meán as it is known in Gaelic, is situated half way between Rosegreen and Fethard. Presently there are fifty followers and the number of subscribers is limited to those who live in the country.

The 1998 opening meet of the Tipperary took place in Fethard on 26th October. It was a cool brisk day with a strong breeze. The breeze swept the white clouds from the sky and for most of the time there was bright autumn sunshine with blue skies. Hundreds of people including families with children had gathered in the square of the medieval town to view the annual spectacle.

The master and huntsman were dressed in their red coats and there were about one hundred followers on horseback from the very young to the more experienced. There were children who were no more than seven years old and there was one elderly gentleman who was eighty-four years young. Some of the followers wore black riding caps while others wore bowler hats. One particular lady caught my attention as she was riding side-saddle.

There was the traditional stirrup-cup of sherry and the hounds and riders were very evidently excited with the prospects of a good chase. Both hounds and riders were blessed before they departed and a prayer was said

To Hunt, Shoot and Stalk

Donie Barrett with a family of young ferrets (Chapter 6)

To Hunt, Shoot and Stalk

Christmas camaraderie at the Shelton Shoot in 1996. (Chapter 7)

TO HUNT, SHOOT AND STALK

An Maidrín Rua (Chapter 8)

Cearc Coille (Chapter 10)

To Hunt, Shoot and Stalk

Mary O'Regan with a six point sika (Chapter 9)

for the safety of all during the coming season. From my viewing point, it was hard to hear everything over the noise of horseshoes and barking hounds. St. Hubert, who was Bishop of Liege in France, was an avid hunter and is recognised as the patron saint of all hunters. I do not think he was mentioned in the prayers in Fethard.

The horn sounded and the field moved out through the Northern Gate of the medieval walls – walls which had been constructed by the Normans and walls which had seen such famous people as Oliver Cromwell in their time. Some spectators followed on foot, some on bicycles, but the majority in cars and jeeps. We followed in the jeep as we often climbed onto the roof or hood in order to get a better view over the white-thorn ditches which could be up to ten feet high.

The first 'draw' was by the banks of the Clashawley River. This river is about twenty feet wide and is easily forded by horses in some sections. The Clashawley is a tributary of the Anner, made famous by the ballad lines 'She lived beside the Anner at the foot of Slievenamon'. A flock of mallard sprung from the river into the clear blue sky but there was no sign of a fox. We followed in the traffic-jam but after many stops and starts, we elected to abandon the jeep and to walk instead.

We walked at a brisk pace towards Rocklow and took up a vantage point at a stone wall fence. It had rained heavily during the previous week and the going was soft. We saw the master and huntsman riding towards a large copse and five minutes later, the rest of the field arrived. There were twenty to thirty spectators beside us and everybody thoroughly enjoyed watching the horses and riders negotiating the fence. The majority of riders cleared the obstacle but there were some embarrassed faces. One rider cleared the fence but on landing fell into four inches of mud and water on the other side. A grey horse refused at the last moment but his rider took to the air and landed on the far side. Another man fell from his saddle on the near side when his mount refused. A friend of mine captured the stray horse and brought it back to the unfortunate individual whose well pressed outfit was covered in mud. Thrice more the horse refused and to make matters worse for the poor man, many children and teenagers cleared the fence with no hassle at all. One fox was caught in the copse but as is the case with most hunts, neither riders nor spectators saw the kill.

The field moved swiftly cross country so we were unable to follow. We crossed a small stream and took up a vantage point on a nearby hill. The weather was still cool an fresh which made for ideal walking conditions. From the top of the hill we had a panoramic view of the surrounding countryside. To the east we could see the famous Coolmore Stud and Slievenamon. Legend says that Fionn MacCumhail, leader of the Fianna and a great hunter, found his wife here. Translated into English,

Slievenamon means 'mountain of the women'. To the south lie the Comeragh Mountains and the Knockmealdowns. To the west lie the Galtees where I had shot a fallow buck at 7.30 a.m. this very day. The hounds were at least two miles to the north and out of sight. Soon we heard the sound of four hundred horse-shoes approaching. The sound of iron hitting the paved road could be heard for over a mile away. There was a wood underneath us which stretched for four hundred yards. The hounds drew on it but their work was all in vain. If I was put in a fox's place, I would leave the area as soon as I heard the 'clip-clopping' of hooves. Maybe the cute fox who lived there had come to the same conclusion?

The hunters rode up a narrow road with stone walls on either side. The master and huntsman took a right turn into a lane-way and proceeded across open countryside again. It was 3.30 p.m. so my wife, son and I decided to head back towards the jeep as we were feeling peckish and thirsty. Thirty minutes later we were in McCarthy's Hotel in the centre of Fethard. We had a 'deoch' by the wood stove but alas Paul Carberry did not ride into the bar on his horse on this particular occasion. Alex Ferguson, Manager of Manchester United Football Club had been here also but that was on 7th January, 1998.

* * *

Fox hunting on horseback is the one section of venery which seems to attract most attention. Hunt saboteurs have caused serious problems for hunt followers in England. The Criminal Justice and Public Order Act of December 1994 made a new offence of 'aggravated trespass'. This law makes it possible for hunt saboteurs to be arrested. It is a criminal offence to interfere with hunters in the United States when they are engaged in their sport in accordance with the local game laws.

All hunters whether they are shooters, hunting hounds on foot or on horseback do so because it is a leisure activity and part of our natural instinct. Hunting is a traditional heritage which goes back as far as the ancient Greeks and Egyptians. Hunting enthusiasts love the countryside and its wildlife. They do not pollute or destroy the environment and they try to conserve its fauna by the most suitable methods of management.

Ten to fifteen years ago, it was the fashion to wear fox-skin fur coats. Trappers were earning twenty to twenty-five pounds per pelt. Fox hunters thought that the fox population would be decimated but as every hunter knows, this was not the case. The fox population was reduced significantly but the cuter and more adaptable fox bred and as a result, a strong healthy fox graph grew. Very few women or men wear fox coats anymore – some people feel definitely intimidated if they do so. The result is that the number of foxes has mushroomed out of all proportion. A large percentage of urban foxes have mange which leaves them in an emaciated state.

A fox is basically a nocturnal animal. Due to the increase in their numbers, foxes can be seen on the prowl during the day – they hunt by day and as a result, they can be considered diurnal. Many foxes are found dead on the roads as they criss-cross their hunting territory. Young foxes or cubs are often found dead during the late summer and early autumn. Adult foxes are found killed on the highways each winter in greater numbers than they were in the past.

The art of fox-hunting is of great economic benefit to Ireland. Bord Fáilte (The Irish Tourist Board) keeps a special list of hunter horses for hire. A single horse is capable of earning up to one thousand pounds per season. Holidaying huntsmen and women have to hire cars and pay for accommodation and food. Airlines and ferries transport the tourist from all over the world. Horses are almost obsolete as draft animals so their only hope of survival lies in sport and leisure activities. 'Hunters' (i.e. horses) must be bred, sold and bought. Many horses of the hunter type are sold as show-horses or show-jumpers. The value of the non-thoroughbred horses is worth millions of pounds both in the internal and export markets. Feeding hunters is also expensive. A hunter may eat up to fifteen pounds of oats and ten pounds of hay each day. The ancient craft of farriery is kept alive as the horses have to be shod. Horse transporters, horse boxes and trailers must be manufactured to various specifications. Saddles must be crafted and the huntsmen and women must be properly attired.

Under new legislation, a fox cannot be dug-out with terriers once it has gone to earth unless it has been causing problems for the landowner and he wants it killed. When the fox has been dug out in its earth, it is shot humanely with a .32 calibre pistol. Foxes have spread rabies on the Continent as far as the English Channel. They are gassed and poisoned where there is a danger to the human population. Hopefully a well managed fox population in Ireland will never carry or spread such a disease.

Hunting keeps a balance in nature. The strongest survive. Humans are the foxes' only natural predator.

CHAPTER NINE

Sika Deer in Wicklow

County Wicklow is situated just south of Dublin city which is the capital of Ireland. The Wicklow mountains are fifteen minutes drive from the city centre. Wicklow is known as the 'Garden of Ireland' due to its magnificent scenery most of it due to glaciation in the last ice age. The plains of Kildare border Wicklow to the west and the Irish Sea lies to the east. St. Kevin who was a monk during Ireland's 'Golden Age of Learning' lived in Glendalough. His monastery and round tower can be seen there today. The predominant rock in the mountains is granite, but during the 7th, 8th and 9th centuries, gold was found there. Much of this gold was used to make the religious book covers and chalices which can be seen in the Historical Museum in Dublin.

The Wicklow mountains were always home to the Irish red deer, but in the last century (1800's) Lord Powerscourt introduced Japanese sika deer. The sika escaped from the estate and spread out over the mountains. Today they are more numerous than the native red and inter- breed with them causing many hybrids.

The sika is the smallest of the three species of deer in Ireland. It is at home on the open mountain as well as the evergreen and deciduous forests. They cause a lot of damage to the new plantations but they also feed on heathers and grass.

The majority of hunting licences are held by sportsmen who shoot in Wicklow and their main quarry is the sika. Like most deer, the best time to stalk sika is during the rut when the stags lay down their guard due to having other things on their mind. I have hunted sika in February but not during the September rut. Stags are hard to come by but at least the mornings are getting longer.

It was 5.00 a.m. as I drove over the Sally Gap from Blessington. The night was clear and there was a biting east wind that rustled the heather at the roadside. I was hoping to see the eyes of some nocturnal animal but there was nothing to brighten up the night except the frost glistening on the sheltered corners of the road. I arrived in Roundwood at 5.30 a.m., phoned my hunting companion, Paul, who promptly turned up ten minutes later, even though he had got to bed at 3.30 a.m. I followed Paul's jeep and soon we reached his house which is nestled in the foothills of the Wicklow Mountains. The kitchen in 'Grouse Lodge' was warm and homely. I sat down beside the Stanley burner and was welcomed by the only other resident of the house who was awake – a fifteen week old orphan otter. I shared my toast with the otter as he whistled and played like a kitten. At this stage his teeth were well grown and he liked to chew on the knuckle of my thumb. Eventually he was put back into his pen in the corner of the kitchen – an action which he totally disagreed with.

We loaded the jeep and headed for the mountains. As we drove along the road at dawn, we saw two sika stags in a field beside a young plantation. The stags were seventy-five yards out and just looked at us as we stopped. A pick-up truck one hundred yards down the road pressed on his brakes also. 'Lead us not into temptation!' so we continued on to our destination.

We arrived at the forest gate, pulled the barrier across and drove along the rutted track. The area consisted of young and mature conifers, bog or moorland, and open mountain. Out on the bog I could see some red deer herds grazing on the frost-burned grasses. Paul spotted a herd of eight sika with two decent stags. After checking wind direction, we decided to stalk along the road and then approach them through the trees which were about three to four feet high. Going through the trees I spotted a two-year old stag. My companion had a shooting stick made of two – five foot dowling rods pinned together four inches from the top. I placed the .243 in the fork and looked at the animal through the 6 x 42 Smith and Bender scope. The stag did not hold steady and moved off over the brow of the hill. We followed him up slowly but on reaching the crest, we could see that he and his companion had moved out of range onto the open mountain.

To my right I saw a herd of twelve sika about eight hundred yards away. Twenty yards to their right was a six point stag whistling and moving upwind outside of a mature plantation. I decided to go downhill and then to follow a gully which should keep me out of sight. The stream in the gully would hopefully drown out any sound.

On my way down hill I stepped in a bog hole up to my knee. The freezing water filled my wellington and I gasped for a second with the cold. My hands were numb as I didn't take my gloves with me – The Golden Vale is a milder and more sheltered spot than a mountain top in Wicklow. I proceeded up the gully for five hundred yards and I could hear the stag whistling but I could not see him. One hundred yards further on, I could see the females but no stag. After another fifty yards I came out of the gully where there was a clear view of the mountain and the plantation to the right. One hundred and fifty yards out I saw a hind but no sign of the stag. I went on but all I saw was the main herd two hundred yards distant on the open mountain. At some stage he must have crossed in front of me as I later heard him whistling in the forest.

Paul had waited on the track so I headed back in what I thought was the correct line. I lost my bearings and there was no sign of my guide! I stepped into more bog holes and he slept in the heather due to the late hour he went to bed.

Our next plan of action was to go up a small valley towards a very young fir plantation which was growing in a grassy glen. Three-quarters of a mile away, we saw a big herd of sika, one red deer hind and four fine stags. We moved up the valley keeping the stream on our left and the sheep fencing on our right. Four hundred yards away we could see the four stags – two eight pointers but the red hind was in between us. After another short trek, we crossed the sheep fencing but we could not move in for the shot as the terrain was too open. Up and up we went and all I could see was the top of the bare mountain with a dusting of snow. Again we crossed the sheep fencing with a small knoll in front. Paul said that this was our only way of having any chance of a shot.

It was decided that I would go forward on my own. I crossed a gully and then began crawling on my knees through the damp heather. When I reached the top of the rise, I looked forward and saw the red hind but no stags. I moved around the rise keeping down wind all the time. Thirty yards further on and the red hind raised her head. She knew that I was there but couldn't see me as I had a camo-mask on my face. Two sika hinds appeared beside her and raised their heads – no sign of the four big stags. Suddenly a two-year old stag raised his head amongst the group. As there was no way of getting to the main objectives without alarming everything, I decided to take my chance. I put the Steyr to the side of a fir tree and put the crosshairs on his neck. At the report the eight pointer broke running from a depression one hundred yards in front. For one instant, he stopped at one hundred and fifty yards but as I was still lying prone a tree blocked my field of view. He took to flight again and was soon out of range. His companions who were further out joined him.

We field dressed the young stag who was in good condition for the time of year. I put on a harness which was made of old seat belt strapping and a piece of rope. I was warm again due to all the adrenalin but I would be warmer by the time I had dragged the animal back down the mountain to the jeep. The old stags are still there and with two weeks left in the season, they should survive to the Millennium rut.

CHAPTER TEN

Timberdoodles and Woodcock

The Irish Punt (£IR) is equal to 100 pence. The heptagonal 50-penny coin bears a picture of a woodcock in full flight on the front. W B Yeats was asked by the Irish Government in the 1920's to design a set of Irish coins. He chose many Irish birds, animals and the salmon. The original coin with the woodcock was a farthing, which was equivalent to ¼ of an old penny. The old Irish /Imperial pound was worth 240 pennies. With the introduction of the metric system and decimalization in the 1970's the Irish pound was worth 100 new pence.

W.B. Yeats won the Nobel Prize for literature but he did not shoot woodcock. Some woodcock stay and breed in Ireland but the majority are winter migrants who come to Ireland for its mild, moist climate. A few birds may be encountered in November but the biggest numbers come from Siberia and Scandinavia when the cold Northeast winds blow – this generally happens around the end of November but not later than Christmas.

The Irish for the woodcock is Cearc Coille – i.e. the hen of the wood. Both sexes are indistinguishable as they have mottled plumage, long bills and short legs and tails which are characteristic of all wading birds. Its diet consists mainly of worms and as a result it is always found in boggy areas. The birds shelter in woodland during the day but flight at dusk to the lowland bogs and marshes and flight back just before dawn. Some birds will remain all day in alder thickets, rhododendron or heavy cover with a stream or creek running through it. Woodcock shooting is best on the West Coast of Ireland stretching from Cork in the South to Sligo and Donegal in the North.

The Woodcock season in Ireland begins on 1st November and ends on 31st January. The 1976 Wildlife Act banned the flighting of woodcock. Flighting of woodcock took place about 15 minutes before dark. The hunters took up position in the flight path between the forest and the lowlands. The birds would come jetting down the mountain slope at maybe

TO HUNT, SHOOT AND STALK

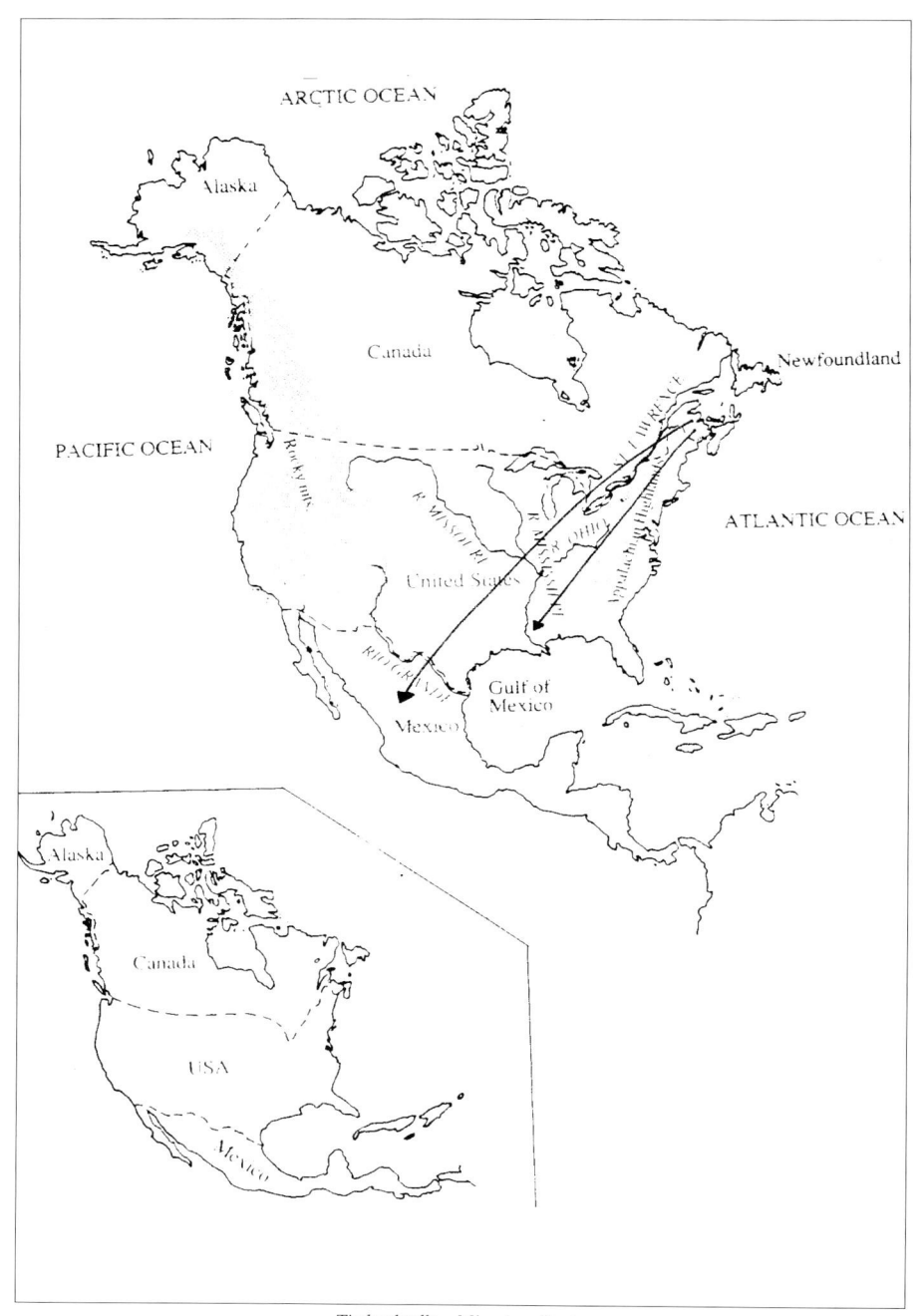

Timberdoodle – Migratory Route

Woodcock – Cearc Coille – Migratory Routes

50-70 mph depending on the prevailing wind. In the late 1960's I saw one gentleman to fire at 15 woodcock but to shoot only one. Any honest flighter would agree that this was par for the course. However the excitement and flow of adrenalin made it all worthwhile.

To the American hunter the woodcock is better known as the Timberdoodle. The Eurasian woodcock is about 35cm or 14' long. The North American bird is slightly smaller and greyish brown compared to the rustic brown of the European bird. The Timberdoodle has to migrate before the ground freezes in order to get his daily diet of worms. A bird from the East Coast of Canada will migrate as far as the Mississippi Valley and Delta. Some birds will go as far as Mexico. The birds travel at night especially when there is a moon. The journey is taken in stages and the birds may stay over in certain areas for a few days. American sportsmen and women will tell you of halycon days when they flushed large numbers of doodles only to come back to the exact location the next day and meet no birds at all. The reason for the drastic change is due to the fact that the birds have all taken flight during the night and journeyed hundreds of miles further south.

The Springer Spaniel is used to hunt woodcock in Ireland. The fearless springer will work hard to flush birds, which are tightly tucked away in heavy cover. The bird does not make any sound when flushed and the only warning you may get is if your shooting companion shouts 'cock'. The bird exits the cover in a waving flight pattern through the trees. The most opportune time to fire is when the bird has reached the top of its rise and is about to level out. An ordinary game gun bored ½ and full with no. 7 or no. 6 hunting load cartridges is ideal for the job. Although the woodcock provides a difficult target it is easily knocked with a few pellets. In Ireland and England the most difficult game shot is considered to be a 'right and left' over woodcock. A brace of woodcock taken with a semi-automatic shotgun will not count. You must also have two witnesses to testify to the fact. If you can provide enough evidence to prove your case a certain drink company will give you a special pin and a bottle of their favourite spirits. I know of one gentleman who was shooting woodcock over Springer Spaniels in Co. Sligo. A pair of woodcock flushed in front of him and he downed his first left and right. The dogs retrieved the birds for the delighted marksman. By some trick of Celtic magic the birds change into two hen pheasants. The misfortunate rough shooter is still trying to play down his fame.

I have shot Woodcock in the state of Maine in the month of October. My companion Mark Carver from Secret Pond Camps in Patten was using a pair of Brittany Spaniels. We hunted in alder thickets, in mixed woodland and around old farms where mother nature was claiming back the land. The farms had long since been abandoned and in the old orchards, which adjoined them, we saw plenty of bear droppings and deer tracks.

The dogs were orange and white in colour and difficult to see at times in the thick fall foliage. A Springer Spaniel would make a crashing sound through the undergrowth but a Brittany Spaniel is quieter. If the dog went out of sight and set you had a problem to find him. The American solution to this was to put a bell on the dog's collar. The bell would 'tinkle-tinkle' as the dog hunted but stopped when the dog set. All you had to do was concentrate on the sound and proceed to where you last heard it.

The most up-to-date version of the bell is to use a collar with an electronic sound emitter. There are various sound emissions but generally the device is set to give off an alarm when the dog comes to point. Apparently this does not upset the bird and certainly not the dog. I use a bell on my Brittany in Ireland for hunting woodcock and pheasant in cover. It doesn't affect either species. The problem I have encountered in Ireland is that the bell can be snipped off in brambles and sometimes the dog may get caught momentarily in briars. Keep your dog within range and concentrate on his location to prevent such occurrences.

When we returned to our log cabin in the evening we were tired and hungry from stepping over blowdowns. We had ten Timberdoodles in the bag and missed as many more. Phil Kenny who accompanied me from Boston was delighted, as he had shot his first woodcock with a 12 gauge single barrel with a hammer action. We drank a few Coors Silver Bullets to celebrate the event beside the old wood stove.

Woodcock are difficult to pluck as their skin is very thin and tears easily. We breasted the birds and fried them up with some moosemeat, which had been shot two weeks previously. Everything tasted delicious. I couldn't detect any difference in my tastebuds between a Timberdoodle and a Cearc Coille.

Chernobyl in Belarus is best remembered for the tragic explosion of its reactor in 1983. The radioactivity in the air was first detected in a monitoring station in Sweden. Ireland has a prevailing westerly wind and this helped to keep most of the radioactive dust away. Sportsmen who shot woodcock in the west of Ireland that year sent them to University College in Dublin to be analysed. The results showed that only two birds contained high levels of radioactivity. The people of Belarus are still suffering the effects of the radioactive contamination but surveys show that woodcock numbers are at a healthy level as we enter the new millennium. However, in 1999 I still know some hunters who will not eat woodcock, as they fear that the flesh may still be contaminated.

CHAPTER ELEVEN

Black Bear in Maine

Bears existed in Ireland before the last Ice Age, which was 10,000 years ago. They would have been similar to the black or brown bears of the North American Continent and the brown bears, which are found in Russia today. The Brown bear found along the coast in Alberta Canada and the Alaskan Panhandle would be a much larger animal because of the abundance of Pacific Salmon. The Kodiak brown bear is the biggest bear in the world. It is found on Kodiak Island in the Alaska Peninsula. These bears can grow to a weight of 1,200 lbs. (600kg). Their huge size is again due to the abundance of game in the island i.e. moose, sitka deer and of course the many species of Pacific Salmon like King, Coho, Sockeye and Chinook.

The bones of our last Irish bears can be found in a limestone cave in the Burren in Co. Clare, which is in Western Ireland. The cave is called the Ailwee Cave and today it is a famous tourist attraction for both the native Irish and internationals. The cave is about 1 hours drive from Shannon International Airport. The cave was formed by underground rivers eroding through the soft limestone rock millions of years ago. The temperature was constant during summer and winter, which made it an ideal hibernating spot. There are no other traces of bears to be found in Ireland today - barring the odd circus or the zoo.

MacMahon is a very common surname in Ireland. It is a true Celtic name unlike names like Fitzgerald or Burke (de Búrca) in Gaelic which can be traced back to the Norman Invaders of 1169 A.D. Mac in Irish means 'the son of'. MacMahon means the son of Mahon. The Gaelic for Mahon is mathún or bear. Therefore the person so called was ' as strong as a bear '. MacMahon is the most common surname in County Clare to this day.

Black bears are still plentiful in the State of Maine, U.S.A. today. The bears may average 1 or 2 to the square mile. Ireland is 32,000 sq. miles in area and Maine is approximately 31,000 sq. miles. Maine is the first state in the U.S., which the sun rises on each morning. It is separated from Canada by the St. Croix River. One of the border crossings is at Calais. New Brunswick is on the other side of the river but it is also 1 hour ahead as it is part of the Atlantic Time Zone.

Maine is not densely populated compared to the other lower 48 states, which make it an ideal spot for wildlife. There are whitetail deer, moose, bobcat, fox, coyote, snowshoe hares, ruffed grouse, woodcock and many species of duck in season. There are always rumours that a mountain lion track has been found and that the cats are slowly moving back to Maine from the West.

The Bear in Maine are mainly black in colour. In Canada the same species can be found in black, brown and cinnamon colour phases. There is only a fall hunting season in Maine but in Canada there may be a spring and fall season depending on what province you may wish to hunt in.

The hunting season in Maine generally begins around the first of September and finishes near the end of October. The dates are set by the Maine Department of Fish and Game each year. In order to hunt in Maine you must have completed a course, which involved gun safety and animal, bird recognition. You must also purchase a big game licence which includes one deer tag (antlered only) and one bear tag. It is a serious offence if the tag is not attached to the animal once it has been shot. A wildlife ranger may inspect your trophy at any time and the animal must be brought to the local game registration station as soon as possible where it can be weighed.

There are two methods of hunting bear in Maine (1) chasing the bear by using dogs. (2) A baited tree stand. When I hunted bear in Maine I chose method one as I like the thrill of the hunt. I went to a friend of mine Mark Carver in Patten, Maine who specialises in the two forms of hunting. Patten is about 1½ hour's drive north of Bangor Maine. Bangor is 5/6 hours drive from Boston or you can fly from Boston to Bangor International Airport in 1½ hours.

Mark runs an outfitting camp called Secret Pond Camps just North of Patten. The camp was built in the 1920's and consists of a number of log cabins with a woodstove, bunkbeds, and shower. All the camps are self-catering so bring your own food and drink. The camp is built in the 'great woods of Maine' which is a mixture of mature coniferous and deciduous trees. Mark does most of his hunting within an hour's drive of the camp

Mark had never met an Irish hunter before. Most of his clients would have been Americans from New York, New Jersey, Pennsylvania and Massachusetts.When I arrived at Secret Pond, Mark had another friend called Ron who had come to hunt bear from a tree stand with a .50 calibre flint-lock musket. They knew by my 'brogue' that I wasn't an Irish – American from Boston. I was offered some Jack Daniels neat and soon the stories flowed. By midnight we knew all there was to know about each other. I adjourned to my bunk and crept into my sleeping bag. I began to dream about Grizzly Adams when I heard a knock at the cabin door.

It was 5a.m. and Mark was calling me to get up to go hunting. I made an ordinary Irish breakfast – Cornflakes, orange juice, boiled egg and tea. I put on my light camouflaged fatigues, wild Turkey Federation baseball cap and leather boots. As a sidearm, I had my original 14' Bowie knife. The gun I had taken was a Winchester .3030 lever action made by Marlin with 170-grain bullets. The gun was a centennial commeration model, which I had bought second-hand in Boston. It had a brass medallion inlaid in the stock and a brass saddle ring like the original cowboy model. The gun was cocked by either pressing down the lever action or pulling back the hammer. Great care had to be taken as each time you loaded a cartridge the gun was cocked. There was a thumb piece fitted at right angles to the hammer, which gave a better grip. The cartridges were Remington round tipped which cost about $12 for a box of 20.

We loaded all the gear into a Chevy Long Cab 4 by 4 pickup. I think that the engine was a 4.1 litre petrol – petrol being about 75cents a gallon. Behind the cabs were 5 wooden dogboxes for the hounds. We had 4 dogs, which were specifically trained for hunting bear and bobcats. Their ancestors would have been beagles and foxhounds. Mark called them Tans andBlue Ticks depending on the colour. They would be similar in size to the Tipperary Foxhounds.

The top of the 'Kennel' was covered in carpet and in the centre there was a ring and chain – this was for the strike dog. The strike dog would travel on top of the platform and scent the bear as we drove along. If a scent was detected the dog would howl and alert Mark and I who were inside the cab.

Mark decided to try some Beech Ridges as the bears feed in these areas in September in order to build up a thick layer of fat for hibernating during the long cold Maine winter. During the months of July and August, Mark had scouted the area for bear tracks and 'scat' i.e. dung. If he thought that a bear was following a particular trail he would bait the area. The bait he used was old donout batter oil mixed with stale sliced pans. This mixture was placed in a two-gallon plastic bucket and securely wired to a tree. Bears have a great sense of smell and can detect the bait from over a mile. If a bear had been feeding in the area recently the strike dog should be able to scent him.

As the Chevy rolled down the forest road I felt a bit hung-over from the Jack Daniels. Every rut and pothole seemed to rattle in my head. Mark pointed to a cow moose feeding in a pond about 120 yards from the road. She didn't seem too perturbed and just kept a watchful glare at us. Moose are scarce in Maine so there is a lottery system if you wish to hunt them. Only the bulls may be shot. A mature adult bull is the same size as a horse.

The locals in Maine use a .270, .308 or 30.06. The important thing to do is to shoot your animal close to an accessible track or else you are in for a lot of hard labour.

Suddenly the strike dog barked to indicate that there was a bear in the area. It was 6a.m. and we had been only ten minutes in the forest, a little too good to be true. We decided to keep on going again as we thought it was a false alarm. We drove about 75 yards on when the dog howled again. This time Mark stopped the truck and decided to let out one of the other dogs to see if there was a genuine trail.

The hound picked up a scent immediately and disappeared about 50 yards into the tall pines. He began to give tongue so Mark decided to release all the dogs. There was a hell of a hullabaloo as all 4 dogs came upon the bear that apparently had been resting up after feeding on bait which had been set in the area. There was a slight altercation between the bear and the pack before the bear exited his bed in a hurry. They all headed deep into the pines and into swampland, which was too dangerous for humans to follow.

All was not lost however as all four dogs had three collars each. An ordinary dog collar, which was removed as soon as they were untethered. A red luminous collar to enable the drivers of the logging trucks to see the dog and to avoid accidents. The most important collar was a tracking telemetary collar with a 3" aerial and a range of a mile. Mark a had a portable aerial similar to those seen on Nature Programs. He also had a small receiver that was about the size of a standard camera. We could hear the dogs barking as they moved south so we decided to follow as best we could by driving along the logging roads.

After five minutes we ran into another problem. The Chevy developed a ' flat' or puncture in the rear wheel. We had to use a 6-foot high manual jack to put on the spare. Even the nuts on the spare wheel took time to remove. Twenty-five minutes had elapsed before the truck was roadworthy again. We had no idea where the dogs were and even the tracking device couldn't pick up a signal. The dogs and bear were probably out of range or else a ridge or hill was blocking the signal.

We drove along for an hour constantly getting out to see if we could hear any sound. Mark climbed up on the cab of the truck and moved the antenna through 360 degrees in the hope of picking up some signal. At one stage we picked up a faint signal so we decided to go down into the wood and the thick undergrowth. Mark took a pack – basket, a saw, axe and some knives. If the bear was large we would have to butcher him on the spot and then skin and 'pack' the meat out. After a mile of breaking through brush the signal died out. A Bull Moose could be heard thrashing his antlers against a tree in a distant swamp but not the slightest sound of a dog baying or howling.

We decided to drive down an old abandoned logging road that made its way behind a beech ridge. Maybe the bear might have denned in a cave behind the ridge and the signal was being blocked for the same reason. The road was at this stage narrower than the pickup and the alders on each side had made an almost impenetrable tunnel. Mark slipped the Chevy into four wheel drive as we slid along the damp rutted track. When the 'path' seemed half as wide as the Chevy we ground to a halt. Mark tried all the manoeuvres of a competent off-roader but nothing seemed to give the wheels a grip. We got out and discovered that we bottomed out; the truck was resting on the chassis and the wheels were spinning in mid-air.

I tried putting stones and logs under different wheels but they were just thrown out again. We had a manual winch, which we tied to the nearest available tree. We pulled it out of the ground and broke two more trees. They were young trees and the ground was very soft. The more mature trees were out of range of the cable or else in the wrong position to give proper leverage. As I put tension on the cable I was always aware that too much pressure could cause it to snap with devastating results for the person caught in the whiplash.

Finally we decided to use the six-foot jack again. We jacked up the rear of the truck first and built a road under the wheels. Then we tried to jack up the front but the jack kept sinking into the soil or tipping over on either side. After a lot of sweat and cursing our 'road' was finally built. The Chevy had just one chance to get out of here and that was in reverse. We said our prayers, slipped the automatic transmission to R and never stopped till we reached a decent gravel road.

Mark set the various dials on the receiver again, rotated the antenna clockwise and anti-clockwise and lo and behold there was the faintest 'beep' towards the east. We drove down the road for about three-quarters of a mile with the antenna out the cab window and the receiver on the seat between both of us. The beeps kept getting louder so we knew we were in business.

Mark stopped the truck and called the dog whose set signal was registering. Whistles are not used and each dog collar has its own particular setting. Two minutes later Dan who was one of the younger dogs appeared from the side of the forest. He was panting hard, but you must remember that it was almost four hours since we last had contact with the dogs and we had driven about 60 miles in different directions during the intervening period. Upon examination Mark noticed bear dung in his collar and around the front of his mouth. Apparently he must have caught up with the bear, the bear would have turned and swung his paw at him before exiting the scene again. This probably happened a few times but eventually the dog tired and gave up the chase . The temperature was in the 70's and it was rather humid. Bears can also run at 40-45 miles per hour.

We had one dog back in the truck kennel but we had no bear and three dogs were still missing. At this stage Mark had a hunch as to where the dogs might be. If we had the luck of the Irish the bear should be there also. Mark was convinced at this stage that we were dealing with a large, cute mature bear. He decided to drive back about 3 miles and to go down a cul-de-sac. At the entrance to this dead end, Mark tried to get a signal and sure enough there was a reading from the other dogs. When we could drive no further we stepped out and sure enough we could hear the odd faint howl in the distance. It was hard to discern as the woodpeckers drowned out most sounds in their constant search for insects. Mark reckoned that the dogs had the bear 'treed' or trapped somewhere towards the East at a distance of ½ mile to a mile.

We got the pack basket ready again and this time I checked the .3030 to see that it was loaded and ready for action. As we made our way through the young alders and beech trees I did not know what to expect. We could hear only one dog 'Gus' give the odd howl. Mark used to shout back at the dog to reassure him that we were on our way. Mark said he was worried about the other two dogs. Maybe they had been badly injured or even killed by the bear. On the other hand they might have been unable to bark being so exhausted after a long day.

Directly in front of us we could hear Gus the oldest and most experienced of the dogs. He was trying to guide us in by barking every few minutes. Mark turned to me and asked if I was OK as this was the first time I would come face to face with a wild bear. I had practised at life-size 2-D targets and it was always at the head or neck. A bear shot in the lungs may travel on for a long time as the layer of fat which can be up to 2½ inches thick can seal the entry wound.

Mark explained that judging by the sound the bear was up in a tree. The dogs would have to be put on leads in case the bear came down and attacked them or in case they might be badly mauled by the bear if he was only wounded by the shot. As we broke our way through the undergrowth, I could see Gus at the bottom of a 75-foot pine tree. The other pair of dogs was 25 yards further back. In a fork at the top of the tree I could see a huge black bear. Mark edged forward to put two of the dogs on a leash. I had the rifle ready but would not shoot until the dogs and Mark were safely back. There was no telescopic sight on the rifle only standard open iron sights. The gun was a brush-buster for use in such circumstances. I had the sights raised to 75 yards and I was confident of the rifle at similar distances. I aimed at the bear's head and pulled the trigger while standing offhand. There was a resounding thump and the bear fell to the ground without even twitching a muscle. The headshot had dispatched him instantaneously. 'Dead' bears have seriously mauled many hunters. Professional guides and experienced hunters always carry a side arm when bear hunting. Mark carried a nickel-plated .44 magnum with plastic grips. He shot the bear again to be completely safe from any mishaps. The .44 cartridge fires a 220-grain bullet and unless you grip the gun properly a shooter can split the webs in his or her hand.

The bear was a large boar weighing 350 lbs. He was 30 years old and his teeth were almost completely worn away. He probably could have survived one more Maine winter if he was lucky. He was having problems foraging already and this was the reason he had come for the bait the previous night or morning. He had his 'summer' coat on. Bears grow a thicker coat later in the autumn before they hibernate. My first impression on seeing the bear was to remind me of a pig – apparently there is some connection between the species. The tail is almost non-existent and the eyes are very small compared to a deer. I tried to lift the front paw but it took two hands and great effort to do so.

If the bear had been average size we would have gralloched him and packed him out. However, Mark realised that we had a trophy bear so it was decided to take him out the way he fell. We tried to move him between the two of us but it was all in vain. After many fruitless efforts we decided to go back to camp and get help from Ron or whoever else was available.

We put a tracking collar on top of the bears back to make it easier to locate on our return. It took us more than an hour to find the Chevy, which was parked at the end of the cul-de-sac. We drove back to camp and located Ron who was excited with the thought of actually seeing the bear. There was no one else available at such short notice so we headed back immediately as the evening was drawing in fast.

All three of us followed the signal back to the bear. It would have been like looking for a needle in a haystack otherwise. We still couldn't move the bear until I decided to cut down a small tree with my Bowie knife and to prop the bears front paws and head on it. Ron then secured the paws with a dog leash. I was wearing two leather belts so I wrapped one around each of the back legs. Mark and Ron would carry the front and I would carry the rear.

The load was so heavy that we could only move 20 feet at a time. We had to move our way around trees, saplings and over countless blowdowns. Luckily we were in the shade and we had no extra weight to carry except the clothes on our backs. At one point we stood in a hornets nest and I am positive that we moved 50 feet as fast as lightning. The mosquitoes were beginning to come out now but we were moving just fast enough so they didn't zero in on our exposed skin. Every five minutes we took a breather and listened to the moose deep in the swamps. When we stopped panting we could hear the odd twig breaking about 200 yards behind in the thick brush. The coyotes knew that there was a free meal to be had. If the bear had been left in the woods over night there wouldn't be much left in the morning – it would remind you of Ernest Hemingway's famous novel 'The Old Man and the Sea'. One and half-hours later we got back to the pick-up. We lowered the tailgate and put the bear on the flatbed. We were dehydrated but Mark was well prepared and took out a six pack of Coors Silver Bullet Beer. I think that this can of beer was the nicest I ever drank in the U.S.A.

Our next stop was in Patten where the bear was weighed and officially tagged. He had to be put on a potato trolley in order to be moved. He weighed 350 lbs. The only other bear shot that week weighed 75 lbs. We drove back to the camp and Mark eviscerated the boar. He was then pulled up on a pulley and tied to the game pole.

I was so exhausted that I cannot remember what I did next. It was now 8.30p.m. and we had been up since 5.00a.m. I awoke in the morning to the sound of many voices and pick-ups and jeeps coming and going. I peered through the small window of the log cabin and there was a crowd of 30 hunters all clad in their camo-outfits admiring the bear. I was still so tired that I did not feel like answering 100 questions. Mark did all the P.R. work. All of them were hunting bear for the week and so far they hadn't seen any sign.

Mark skinned the bear, salted it and put it into the freezer. It would be sent to California to be tanned and then back to Skowhegan to be lined and made into a rug. The meat was quartered, as it would be the easiest way to transport it. Bear meat is dark but it is very tasty if made into sausages or burgers. Like beef the younger the animal the better it tastes. Orientals consider the gall bladder an Aphrodisiac but that is a story better told at another time.

CHAPTER TWELVE

Whitetail Deer

The whitetail deer is a native of North and South America. It can be found from Sasketchwan in Canada to the foothills of the Andes. The term whitetail deer comes from the white colour on the underside of the deer's tail. The tail is also called a 'flag' and it is used to warn other deer of danger and to make it easy for a fawn to follow a doe. Indeed it is the flag and the white rump area which hunters generally see.

The whitetail is both a grazer and a browser. Numbers are smaller in the northern states but the animals are bigger. There were forty million whitetail deer in North America before colonisation. Their number dropped to less than half a million during the twentieth century due to over-hunting and destruction of their habitat. There are about fifteen million today due to proper game laws. The coat is predominantly brown but the young have a white speckled coat to hide in dappled forest sunlight. A whitetail may live from ten to twenty years and weigh from one hundred to four hundred pounds. Ask an Irish hunter what his or her main quarry is and the answer will usually be 'Pheasant'. The American answer is always the Whitetail deer. Pursuit of the whitetail in the U.S. is like a ritual. The season for deer hunting in Ireland is six months. September to February for bucks or stags, and November to January for hinds or does. In many areas of the States, the rifle season for bucks may last only four weeks and you may be allowed shoot only one antlered animal. However you may extend your season as there is an archery season before the rifle season and a black-powder season afterwards. In some areas which have become very built-up, a shotgun is the only weapon allowed.

The black-powder guns have become so modernised now that they are almost black-powder in name only. Some models can carry telescopic sights and the barrels are rifled. Most of the large shotgun manufacturers provide a second barrel which is rifled and machined to take a scope. Many shotguns are made specifically for deer hunting and come in a large variety of finishes using wood and synthetic materials.

A large number of hunters live in urban areas so they generally only get one chance a year to go deer hunting. Eleven months of the year may be given over to preparing for the November rut and the chance of a heavy buck with a massive rack. This massive rack can be measured on the Pope and Young or the Boone and Crockett scale to see if it will have world record status. Deer hunters buy all sorts of camo clothing which would equal the best used by an army sniper. Blocking and attracting scents of all types are used; you may buy a scent which resembles the doe in estreus: place the scent on pads on your boots and hope that the biggest buck you ever saw comes charging in to you. Tree stands are also very popular in America. One particular company gives a free video of trophy hunts to promote its products. There are permanent tree stands and the lighter more portable variety which can be carried and set up anywhere. Stands may vary in price from one hundred and twenty five dollars to five hundred dollars.

Calls are also used to attract the deer. Grunt calls are used to annoy the buck during the rut. Hopefully his aggression will get the better of him, he will drop his guard and come to investigate who is trespassing in his territory. I have tried Whitetail grunt calls in Ireland for fallow deer. The animals did not answer back or come running to me. However, I have had bucks step out of cover to see what was making the noise and I got shots which I never would have in other circumstances. There are also calls which make the sound of a doe or the distress sounds of a fawn.

Rattling is another method used to attract bucks. It consists of rattling a set of antlers together to imitate two bucks with their antlers locked in mortal combat. The best method here is to rattle every two to three minutes for about ten seconds. Alternatively you may thrash a tree with the antlers to simulate a deer trying to get rid of velvet off his antler. Fibre glass models of antlers can be bought in stores or a rack belonging to a small buck can do just as well. Be careful where you hang the antlers when you go into the woods. Some hunters carry them on a chord suspended around their necks. Always remember that a trigger happy individual may mistake you for a deer.

During rifle season you must wear a certain amount of fluorescent clothing – in some states the minimum square area is stated in the regulation booklet. I used to wear a sleeveless net vest and a fluorescent peaked cap. Many garments can be worn both ways – one side with standard camouflage markings and the inside lining in fluorescent markings. Safety is a paramount factor. During the six months of the deer season in Ireland, I have met on average one hunter in the same area. I hunted during Thanksgiving in Maine and during the first two and a half hours I counted twenty-eight hunters. With such hunting pressure, there is always danger from the inexperienced hunter or the guy who shoots first and asks questions later. You can buy camo-fluorescent toilet paper or or camo designed underwear. There is no point in getting shot in the butt if you are answering a call of nature! In the New England States, the typical topography of the land consists of a mixture of deciduous and coniferous trees interspersed with farmland. Many areas may be inpenetrable due to swamps, beaver dams or the lack of any suitable gravel roads. Parts of Northern Maine may be accessed by being flown in by float plane. No matter where you go in New England you are better prepared if you travel by 4 X 4 jeep or pickup. The Appalachian Mountains which make their way up the east coast of America supply superb habitat for whitetail deer.

Due to the denseness of the forest many shots may be taken at moving targets through heavy brush. 'Brushbuster' rifles are common in these areas, that is, a short barrelled rifle firing heavy grained round tipped bullets. The gun I used was a .3030 Marlin with one hundred and thirty grain nosler partition bullets. Other popular guns were .375 and .444 calibre fitted with Lyman peep sights. My companion, Jared, used a .3006 Remington automatic and a .223 Remington bolt action. Both guns were fitted with wide angle 6.12 X 50 scopes. In some States it is permitted to hunt deer using bolt action handguns. These guns may also be fitted to take a scope or a bi-pod stand. At a range of one hundred yards, they can be as lethal as any rifle.

I have attended centre-fire rifle shooting competitions run by the Southern Deer Society in Munster. Shots are taken at one hundred metres, two hundred metres and three hundred metres standing, kneeling and prone. The first gun club competition which I went to in Maine had a Running Deer Shoot. This consisted of a wooden silhouette of a deer with various scores given for hitting the different sections of the deer, that is, nine points for neck, eight for heart, three points the rump, etc. The 'deer' was on a cable which was moved electronically through the woods. The shooter stood in one position and took two shots. There were only two gaps between the trees where you could get a possible shot. There was nothing to be seen when you called for your deer. You could however hear the deer moving on the pully and judge in what direction it was going. I borrowed a .375 Winchester Magnum lever action with a beautiful octagonal barrel. The first shot missed but the next shot hit the lung area which gave me a score of seven points. Many people do not agree with running shots but the key to survival is always to adapt to your environment. The sights on that particular gun were Lyman peep sights. If a hunter practises with these, he can be as accurate as the person with the telescopic sight. For close shots in thick woodland, a peep-sight will outshine any variable or fixed power scope.

* * *

To Hunt, Shoot and Stalk

The first whitetail trophy I had seen was in my friend Jared's study in Massachusetts. He had shot it in New Hampshire when his grandfather had taken him on a hunting trip. Jared was only sixteen years old at the time and he had shot the deer with a bolt action .223 as it was crossing a trail in the late afternoon. Jared and his father-in-law, Jim decided that they would return to Northern New Hampshire for a week in November 1989. They asked me to go along for the week but I told them that I would be unable to do so until late on Friday. They headed north but promised to keep me informed of events.

There had been hard frosts during the week but neither Jim nor Jared had got a buck. They had seen many does and a few fawns but none of the 'big-boys'. They saw plenty droppings and tracks so they knew that there were many deer in the area. Another phone call on Thursday re-iterated the same story.

On Friday evening Jared's wife, Jackie arrived at our duplex to collect my wife Maria, my son Shane and myself. As we drove north along route 93, clouds were beginning to cross the face of the moon. I had hunted deer previously on frosty mornings in the U.S. and knew how hard it is to move quietly. Due to the large amount of deciduous oak, silver birch and beech, the forest floor is strewn with crispy withered leaves. The result of trying to stalk or still-hunt a deer in these conditions is like trying to walk silently on a kitchen floor covered with cornflakes. The air felt damp and moist outside so hopefully there would be a shower of rain during the night. If so, the ground and leaves would be soft and the only chance of making a sound would be of cracking a twig underneath. I was more familiar with these damp and wet conditions in Ireland and as a result I felt cautiously confident.

The last time I had been in New Hampshire was to go skiing in Waterville the previous Easter. Waterville is only about two and a half hours drive from Boston and is a very popular ski resort with New Englanders. Mount Washington, four thousand, two hundred and eighty-eight feet, is one of the highest points in New England and is a favourite spot amongst hill climbers and those who follow the Applachian Trail. Franconia Notch is a deep chasm carved between the mountains by a previous ice age. It was dark however as we drove but the profile of the peaks could be seen when the moon surfaced from behind the clouds.

We arrived safely at Littleton just as a light mist began to fall. Jim and Jared had still drawn a blank but they had gained a lot of information about the likely hot spots. Jared was worried that with the luck of the Irish, I would bag a fine buck in the first twenty minutes of the morning. He had hunted with me often enough to know that I seldom drew a blank.

We were up and out of bed at 4.30 a.m. All three of us headed for the local café which specialised in hunter's breakfasts. Indeed there were no other crazy people up at this hour except deer hunters. There were two other hunting parties in the café. They had their red tartan type jackets and caps which seemed to be the custom in these areas. Again the main object was to keep warm whereas in Ireland it is to keep dry. No wellingtons here only good insulated boots with proper ankle support. I ate some bacon and eggs with the sunny side up and two cups of coffee. For those who do not understand the American breakfast menu: bacon equals rashers and fried eggs have their sunny side up.

After breakfast we set off for Coos country near Colebrook in Jim's chevy truck. The drive was about forty-five minutes and we discussed strategy on the way. Jim would try some fields at the edge of the woods where he had seen deer grazing on a previous morning. Jared and I would go about a half mile away and into the woods. We would sit up on separate beech ridges in the hope of spotting a buck travelling between eating and sleeping areas. I had no topographic map of the area so I basically hadn't a clue as to where I was. It was still pitch dark and there was only the light of the moon through the clouds to show us where we were going. We had pocket torches but both of us disliked using them in any hunting situation. They are fine for emergencies, and finding gear in the back of trucks, but other than that, they spook wildlife.

Jared pointed to a beech ridge which ran from north to south. It was about seventy-five feet high and about two hundred and fifty yards long. He had seen deer passing close to it on a previous morning. There was a swamp about a half mile away where more than likely some deer sought refuge. Jared told me to stay in position. If either of us got a deer and needed help, we were to fire two shots ten seconds apart when we were sure that the morning movement of deer had finished. Jared then left me to climb the ridge and disappeared to find his own stake-out.

American law states that you cannot shoot deer until a certain time after sunrise or a specific time before sunset. For those hunters who are not sure of the exact times they are printed to the day and the minute in the copy of the state shooting regulations which is provided with every hunting licence. The dawn began to break, there was no breeze and the ground was moist from the rain. The sky was clear and the weather forecast for the morning was good. I was sitting with my back to a tree on an insulated waterproof cushion. Both sides of the ridge were plainly visible and I could cover the entire area within a seventy-five to one hundred yard radius. It was up to the deer to play their part now.

I was hopeful that the first twenty minutes after sunrise would prove fruitful but I saw or heard nothing. No shots came from Jared's direction so he must have been experiencing lean times also. After an hour and a half, I heard a twig snap and turned about to see Jared approaching. He said that a herd of five does passed him soon after dawn but other than that there was no sign of any movement.

We decided to walk slowly through the woods in a circular pattern. We might jump or disturb a deer and maybe one of us might get a shot. If you circle deer they become confused as to your exact intentions and they will not always make a straight exit out of the area. We remained about one hundred yards apart and we could see each other clearly due to our fluorescent jackets. There were many old prints and droppings but we did not rise any deer. The bears were in hibernation now and the only other game we saw was a pair of ruffed grouse and the odd snow-shoe hare which looked like a fleeing deer.

We saw some large fields through the trees about eight hundred yards ahead. We glassed them carefully but there were no deer. There was no sign even in the young trees just bordering the fields. Another hunter made an appearance on a ridge overlooking the farm. We waited to see if he would push some deer forward but our wait was in vain.

I spotted a creek meandering through the fields with a grove about two hundred and fifty yards long on either side. The grove narrowed to about forty yards at the end where there was a crossing into a similar area which joined the main forest. It looked like an ideal area for a deer to rest and also to set up an ambush.

Jared said that he would walk through the grove and that I should wait at the bottom. He gave me ten minutes to get into position before he began his drive. I found a small rocky embankment which gave me a good rest and which provided a good panoramic view of all areas of the grove. Even if a buck bolted from the sides, I should still be able to get a shot. Sometimes Jared tapped the trunks of the trees with a stick in order to startle any deer. He moved in a zig-zag pattern to be certain of hunting most of the likely spots. After fifteen minutes Jared came out in front of me. He saw nothing and neither did I. It was such a suitable place for a hunter that maybe any inexperienced buck who entered it never came out alive again. Wise old bucks always lie in a place where they can exit unnoticed if they feel threatened.

It was now 11.30 a.m. and we must have been about three miles from the pickup. We decided to head back to the east of the area where we had hunted earlier. We worked our way back in a circular pattern going through brush and up and around various ridges. We came into an area where there was a logger's path and where the silver birches, oak and maple were only about eight to ten years old. I noticed a number of tracks in the compost-like soil. There were also some fresh droppings about fifteen feet in from the side of the path. I stopped and knelt down to give a better examination.

Deer had definitely been in this area sometime between dawn and the present.

I stood up and looked down the logger's path. To my amazement, a buck was ambling towards me! Ambling is the only word I can use to describe his progress as he was walking slowly, sniffing the ground sometimes and basically without a care in the world. He never saw me and never even detected my presence. I know my luminous jacket had no affect on him as I was standing on the trail about eighty-five yards from him. I whispered to Jared who was twenty yards to my left and raised my .3030 and waited for the deer to come about twenty yards closer in and to stop. I had open iron-sights on my Marlin lever action. They were set at seventy-five yards. I peered through the rear sight and waited for the deer's bulk to fill it. My breathing began to quicken and I slowly put pressure on the trigger with the pad of my index finger. One shot rang out and he never knew what hit him. Neither of our luminous jackets deterred him but most importantly, we were not walking at the time. I am firmly convinced that it is movement and not colour which frightens deer.

He was a two and a half year old buck. Maybe he had been pushed out of the area by a bigger animal. Again we may have moved him during our morning trek through the woods. It took us about an hour to drag him back to the truck. Jared had been a college body-building champion so this took a little bit of the pressure off me. Things got tough when we reached the main logging road as it was badly cut up with rain filled ruts. We met the local farmer on whose lands we were hunting and after a long cordial chat, he said that there was no problem in driving into the wood to collect the deer.

Jim was waiting at the truck when we returned, however he was deerless. He had got a good chance at a big buck just after first light in the fields bordering the forest. He was using a bolt action .243 which he hadn't hunted with for a number of years. He had only a few old cartridges and he was unable to buy any of that calibre in the area. To make a long story short, Jim put the crosshairs on the buck's chest and pulled the trigger. The gun misfired, the buck heard the click, raised his head and was never seen or heard of again by any of us.

We returned to the motel, and then to the local game registration station. The buck weighed one hundred and seventy-five pounds and was a nice six pointer. There were four other bucks taken in the area on that particular day. They were about two to three years old on average, but all were in great physical condition. There would be an ample supply of steaks for the coming year.

Everybody went to an antique fair in the afternoon and then for a sumptuous surf and turf dinner that evening to celebrate. As we left the restaurant, it began to snow heavily. We were in the poet Robert Frost's country. I was reminded of the lines we learned in High School in his poem *'Stopping by woods on a snowy evening'*.

>"These woods are lonely, dark and deep,
>But I have promises to keep,
>And miles to go before I sleep
>And miles to go before I sleep"

We had two hundred and fifty miles to drive the following day so we all adjourned to bed early.

It was Sunday so we drove south along route ninety-three. Many vacationers and hunters were on the move after the weekend. It was easy to recognise the hunters from the holiday-makers or skiers. They were the ones with all the hunting gear in the back or with a buck on the roof-rack or protruding from the boot. New Hampshire game regulations state that some part of an animal must be visible if you are transporting it. A good and efficient way of reducing poaching but maybe it could upset some people's feelings!

CHAPTER THIRTEEN

Flighting Canada Geese

The Canada Goose is the main quarry for Massachusetts wildfowlers. The season may be broken up into two or three sections depending on the number of geese available. The first section begins in the early fall for about three weeks. Another is just before Christmas, and the last is generally around the end of January and the beginning of February. Wildfowlers need a state licence and a migratory wildlife stamp. Part of the money from this stamp goes towards conservation. Wild fowlers pursue the geese on the marshes, corn fields, or on the open sea.

The geese begin to migrate south from Canada about September. They continue to do so for about two or three months. They have bred during the late spring and summer in the tundra areas of Northern Canada. Instinct tells them that the wet lands will soon freeze over and that there will be no food available. The geese which migrate to the shores of Southern Massachusetts follow the Atlantic flyway. There are a number of other flyways; the Mississippi, Central and the Pacific. The majority of the geese which follow the Atlantic flyway do not remain. They stop over for various periods of time before flying south to areas such as the Chesapeake Bay and other southern locations. Be that as it may, there are thousands of geese to be found in Massachusetts. Golf courses can easily prove this point. The geese love to graze on the succulent grass but they also ruin the areas with their droppings. Many geese never migrate back to the northern zones of Canada. Apparently because of the abundant supply of food they remain in the state like the resident wildfowl population.

My friend, Jared lived in Southern Massachusetts near New Bedford which is on the coast. New Bedford is a famous fishing port but owes its original prosperity to the whaling ships of the last century. Part of the film 'Moby Dick' was filmed here and the famous church where the sermon scene was filmed can be visited by tourists to this day. Many of the sea scenes were filmed in Youghal in County Cork in Ireland. There is a pub there called the 'Moby Dick' which has pictures of Gregory Peck or Captain Ahab on the walls. There are many islands to the south of New Bedford including Nantucket and Martha's Vineyard to the south east. Many of the inhabitants of the New Bedford area are of Portuguese descent but some fishermen from the Aran Islands off the west coast of Ireland have immigrated here in the last number of years.

Jared had relatives who were farmers and their property bordered a river and marsh. The farm was of a mixed variety consisting of dairying and tillage. The main tillage crop was corn, that is, the corn on the cob variety. Flocks of hundreds of geese will land to forage in these fields when the corn has been harvested. If you drive by some fields beside a public road, you are sure to see birds that are never disturbed. Southern Massachusetts is fairly densely populated so it is too dangerous to shoot in many areas. Much of the land is posted or preserved. The farm which we were going to hunt had none of these problems but most importantly it wasn't under too much hunting pressure as only Jared and his cousin were allowed to shoot there.

There was a daily bag limit in the specific coastal division in which we would hunt. Jared had been filling his limit every day when he telephoned for me to come for a shot on Saturday morning. I was looking forward to the experience as I had never shot geese before. Goose shooting in Ireland had been banned and anyway the area which I had lived in did not provide a suitable habitat. The bogs of central Ireland provided superb conditions for geese at one time but most of this is now drained and the geese pass over and go to the Wexford slobs instead. At present there is limited shooting in some areas for Canada Geese and Greylags.

When I arrived in Jared's house he showed me a fine 'honker' which he had shot the previous day. He had a one and a half year old chocolate labrador which was showing great potential. The weather was fine and warm; there were flocks of geese and there was still enough food in the cornfields to attract the birds.

The wild-fowlers in this area prefer pump-action or semi-automatic shot guns capable of firing three inch magnum shells. I had seen mini-magnums in Ireland but these cartridges looked enormous. Even as I write, three and a half inch magnums are being manufactured. Twelve, ten and eight gauge guns with multiple chokes are the favourite weapons. The most important rule to remember in the coastal area is that you have to use steel shot. You must also have a gun which is capable of firing steel shot without damaging the barrel. All shotguns manufactured in the U.S. today are capable of firing steel shot and many new European guns can fire steel shot also. However, whether the gun is of American or European origin, it is best to check with the manufacturer or a reputable gun-smith and have it proof tested.

If you have used No. 4 lead shot you ought to drop to No. 2 steel. The pellets are naturally lighter, and their ballistics are completely different. I remember firing at a Bufflehead with steel shot (similar in size to a teal) which was crossing from left to right along a river. The pellets struck the water about four feet over the duck. I remember saying to Jared that it was like firing feathers at the birds. Steel shot was introduced in coastal areas to prevent lead poisoning by birds injesting the spent pellets. Personally I have never seen any birds displaying strange characteristics which may or may not have been caused by lead. Unless wild-fowlers use a lower number cartridge and shoot at a closer range, many birds will be injured and escape as a result of the change to steel shot.

The last time I bought steel shot it was nearly three times as expensive as lead. Wildlife rangers may check your cartridges to make sure that you are actually carrying the proper loads. The use of steel shot is due to be made mandatory in the European Union in the early Millennium.

We awoke at 4.30 a.m. the following morning and went to a local café for breakfast. In many areas of the States you can get a hunter's breakfast. When wild-fowlers or hunters travel long distances from other States, they always need some sustenance to get them through the day. Try finding a café or restaurant in Ireland which opens at four o'clock in the morning. There were two groups of fowlers there. One group had their own camouflaged duck boat piled high with decoys. Jared explained that they would be hunting out on the open sea all day. It looked as though there wouldn't be too much pressure on the geese in our area today.

When we arrived at the cornfield it was still dark. We drove the Toyota 4x4 pickup down by the side of a ditch which divided the field from the marsh and river. We took out our decoys and set them in a v-formation about forty yards out from the ditch. There was only the slightest breeze but we placed them facing the wind. In all we had about forty magnum birds – some were sitting, more standing, and one or two 'look-outs' to the side. Then we built our net blind and placed all our gear inside. Finally Jared drove the pickup back to the farm and hid it behind one of the out-buildings – hopefully everything would look normal to the Canadas!

There was a nice cool breeze coming off the marsh to our rear. The sun was beginning to rise and there were no clouds in the sky except for an early morning fog bank lying over the marsh. The geese hadn't lifted from their roosts yet and all was quiet.

After twenty minutes we heard the geese somewhere back towards the North-West. In the clear still morning it sounded as though they were three miles away. If we were lucky maybe they would come our way. Jared spotted a huge skein of about five hundred birds flying South about one mile to the West of the farm buildings. We both began to 'honk' on our wooden calls. Jared was an expert due to plenty of practise but these geese had their sights set on some other cornfield. I was disappointed but it was short lived. A flock of one hundred and twenty birds was flying about five hundred yards from our position. We 'honked' with all our lungs and the geese began to answer. The lead bird banked and a flock of about fifty began to turn and circle. They saw our decoys in the field and were intent on joining them. We got ready for action as the birds were nearly within range. Alas there was an unexpected 'Whoosh' behind us and the geese flew away in alarm. We had been so preoccupied in looking in front that we never noticed what was happening behind. Floating or flying on the far bank of the river over the marsh was a hot-air balloon. It was only one hundred feet from the ground and the sound was made by the burner. The air was so still at this stage that the balloon seemed to be hanging in the one spot. I thought at one stage that the flying apparition would plummet into the swamp. After a few more 'Whooshes' he sailed away and so did all the geese.

We licked our wounds, drank more coffee and decided to 'jump' some duck along the river. Things had settled down now and there were no U.F.O.'s in the area. The first place we tried was a small inlet which was surrounded by reeds with an open area on one side. There was a number of boulders here so we would have some cover to hide our approach. As we raised our heads a solitary black duck sprang from the edge of the reeds and was quickly dispatched by Jared. The chocolate labrador dived in and retrieved him gently to hand. As we walked through the reeds in another area, I saw two buffle-head coming low over the river in my direction. I crouched down in the mud and waited till the birds were crossing in front of me. This time I knew what type of lead to give with the steel shot and it wasn't long till the Lab was swimming again.

I had never seen a black duck up close till today. It is similar in size to the mallard. The markings are a duller brown and the duck and drake look basically the same. The main difference between a mallard and a black duck is the bars on the wings called the speculum. A mallard has white stripes on the sides of the bars where as these are absent in the black duck. We were standing in the reeds which were on average six feet high when we heard a sudden 'honk'. I looked up and there was a small flock of twenty geese coming straight at us. We crouched down and dared not look up in case our faces would alert them. As the sounds were almost directly above us, we sprang to our feet and opened fire. Two birds fell to the ground within twenty feet of where we stood. They were young birds weighing ten pounds and twelve pounds respectively. It was 11.30 a.m. now and the temperature felt like 20°C (68°F). We decided to head for home as we were more than satisfied with our bag.

* * *

The next occasion I went goose hunting was in the month of December. The temperature in the early morning and evening was about +20°F excluding the wind chill factor. If you are going to flight geese in these conditions, you need thermal underwear, layers of clothes, a baraclava to hide and keep your face warm, and of course well insulated gloves. Most of the camo gloves had special features for the trigger finger. We always took plenty of flasks of hot coffee to keep heart and soul alive.

Five hundred yards behind Jared's house, there was a salt marsh. We knew that there were plenty of geese there, but to get to them was the problem. I had often mentioned using my square stern Canadian canoe though the proposition always seemed to fall on deaf ears. Barry and Jared had been having a lean time of late, so we decided to try the canoe on the following Saturday.

I loaded the canoe on top of my Ford Mercury 4.2 litre and headed south from Boston. It was 3.00 a.m. and there was a hard frost outside. On the sides of the highway I could see banks of frozen snow glistening in the headlights. The roads were well salted but I still took my time.

By 5.00 a.m. I was in Jared's back yard. There were two inches of frozen snow on the ground, and not a puff of wind. We packed paddles, life jackets and food into the canoe and began the long portage. The route was through four hundred and fifty yards of forest from Jared's back lawn. We crossed dykes, streams and gullies. I couldn't imagine doing this in the Fall before all the undergrowth had been burned off by the heavy frosts of early Winter. I had portaged in the Liffey Descent race back home in Ireland but this was more like the Route de Voyageurs which the early French had used to cross Canada. The most difficult part however lay ahead. Just between the forest and the edge of the reeds, there was an area of thick slimy mud dotted with blow-downs and rotten trees. We tried to keep the canoe's momentum going – Barry pulling the rope at the front and Jared and I holding the gunnels to keep her on a level keel. Rather than make the canoe lighter by taking out its cargo, we kept going in order to save time. The boat came to a sudden halt when it struck a hidden tree stump. Jared and I fell to the side but Barry who was straining forward was tugged backwards by the sudden stop. He gave out a low painful groan and had to stop for five minutes. We decided to unload the canoe and drag it to the river and then come back for all the gear. We had only seventy-five yards to go and the dawn was still about twenty minutes away.

Eventually we reached the river and loaded the equipment once again. Jared decided to paddle out with me to the tail of an island where two streams met. He would lay out the decoys and I would return and collect Barry who was feeling a slight twinge of pain in his lower back at this stage.

To Hunt, Shoot and Stalk

Bear hounds with strike dogs on top (Chapter 11)

Black bear rug (Chapter 11)

To Hunt, Shoot and Stalk

One of the log cabins at Secret Pond Camp (Chapter 11)

Mark at the Game-Pole (Chapter 11)

To Hunt, Shoot and Stalk

Whitetail Does and Fawn with summer markings (Chapter 12)

New England Whitetail Buck taken with a 30.06 Remington Semi-Automatic (Chapter 12)

TO HUNT, SHOOT AND STALK

The author with a large Canada Goose (Chapter 13)

The Andrea-Dory making its way through the swamp (Chapter 13)

The canoe had a square stern and I generally used a one and a half H.P. Evinrude to power along. The engine would have been too heavy to carry through the woods so it remained in the trunk of the car. The current wasn't strong however, so I made good progress.

By the time I arrived back with Barry, there were decoys floating below the point of the island and more were sitting and standing on the marsh on both sides of the main river. They looked very inviting to me and hopefully they would have the same effect on the Canada geese. We towed the canoe up on the island and placed it on its side in the mud. We covered it with reeds and brush and soon had a perfect makeshift hide.

Though it was about 20°F we didn't feel the cold due to all our exertions. It was still fairly dark so we had a mug of coffee to calm the nerves. We heard the odd goose in the distance but there were still no birds to be seen.

Just after dawn a large flock of geese lifted in the distance but they did not come our way. We knew that some birds had to pass over us at some stage because there was a farm opposite Jared's house where about two hundred to four hundred geese fed every day. The land was posted or preserved so the birds were never disturbed. We were directly positioned on their flight line so we should see some action if we had patience.

Teal whizzed past us offering some tempting shots but we resisted. We waited for two hours after daybreak but we still hadn't fired at a goose. I was frozen to the core and Barry was looking for paracetamol to ease the pain in his back. There was no protection out here and the breeze was beginning to strengthen.

Just as our spirits were at their lowest, we spotted a small skein of fifteen birds coming down the marsh. They were following the stream and had heard our calls. They spotted the decoys and six birds came in for a closer look. When they were within range we opened fire. I knocked one down in front and so did Jared. Barry had one bird down in the marsh twenty yards behind. We didn't have the labrador this time so Jared and I launched the canoe to pick up the two birds which were floating motionless in the water.

Everything quietened down again and after another hour we decided to gather our belongings and depart. The three geese were mature birds and my bird weighed twenty-one pounds. I later put him in the freezer and had him for the Christmas dinner. Barry did not fare out too well as things turned out. He either pulled a muscle in his back or pinched a nerve. He went to his doctor the same evening and was out of work for the following three weeks. We never went out on the marsh again in the canoe. The name embossed on the metal square-stern was the Andrea-Dory. Apparently the Andrea-Dory was the name of a ship which had sunk off the shores of Cape Cod!

CHAPTER FOURTEEN

Bobcat

It was New Year's Eve as I put the Luighi Franchi 12 bore semi-automatic into the gun case. The two stickers on the case showed a black bear and a whitetail deer. One said 'Maine Vacationland' and the other said 'Maine – the way life should be'. I was hoping that at least it would snow in the Northern State. It was 11 degrees C in Ireland which meant you could walk down the town to celebrate the New Year without wearing a coat.

The C.N.N. weather forecast was for snow in Maine on Tuesday. It was Saturday night so it meant the transatlantic flight from Shannon to Logan in Boston would be unaffected. The most important journey would be from Boston to Bangor, Maine. If there was a sudden blizzard all my plans could be jeopardised. I had purchased thermal socks, underwear (longjohns and vest) and a thick polo-neck sweater. I had my ski-gloves and my duvet jacket also. I wouldn't be wet out there but it could be down to minus 50 degrees Fahrenheit (-10°C).

The Franchi had been stripped down, cleared and oiled. I didn't want anything jamming after travelling 3,000 miles. The gun weighed 6.21 lbs (2.8 Kgs) and due to its lightness produced a heavy recoil. It had been used so much that I replaced two firing pins, one extractor pin and a spring in the safety. It was originally designed as a five shot but it had to be plugged since the 1976 Wildlife Act came into force. I had a permit from the local Garda Siochana and I also carried my gun licence.

The flight on New Year's Day from Shannon was uneventful except from the nagging hangover, which I had developed from the previous night's festivities. There had been lots of hunters in the local hostelry who wanted to give the old season and year a good send off. The forementioned hunters said that they would go out for a shot in the morning but I knew that it was fast asleep they would be instead of traipsing through the mud.

As the 747 flew over Newfoundland I could see the frozen harbours and snow-covered landscape. The clearings between the trees could be identified from 30,000 feet. The rivers looked like snow covered meandering roads. I was hoping to see a moose from where I was sitting but somehow or other I think I was guilty of wishful thinking.

My buddy Jared and his wife were waiting for me in Logan airport. I was going to stay with them down near Cape Cod and then return to Boston the following day to get the connecting flight to Bangor. There was no snow around Boston and only a dusting down near the Cape. We would have gone after Canada geese that day but hunting is not allowed in Massachusetts on Sunday. It is a legal tradition going back some people say to old religious practices. We planned to go shooting as soon as I got a bobcat and returned from Maine. We passed the Sunday afternoon driving a quad (A.T.V.) followed by Jared's daughter Emily who was driving a battery-operated model.

We drove back to Boston the next morning to catch the 12 o'clock flight to Bangor, Maine. If you go through an American airport your gun will often be referred to as a 'weapon'. One of the airport staff asked me what I had in my case. I explained that I had a shotgun and that I was going on a hunting trip. He put the gun-case, which was securely locked through the x-ray machine. He stopped the conveyor belt, as he seemed to get a shock. I walked over to the monitor and saw what was causing the problem. It was a short case so I had removed the barrel and forearm grip from the stock section. The recoil spring on the stock and firing section looked like a machine gun. The attendant called in a state trooper. I explained what was in the case; he looked at the screen never asked me to unlock the case and told me to move on.

The flight to Maine was in a 12-seater propeller plane. It flew at a much lower altitude to a transatlantic jet. There seemed to be a light dusting of snow on the forest floor, the skies were clear and I thought of all the lobster pots, which could be seen of the Rocky Coast of Maine during the summer. George Bush had a summerhouse down there and F.D. Roosevelt had a house further north in Campobello Island. However at this time of year there are very few vacationers in Maine except for skiers, ice fisherman and bobcat hunters.

Mark met me at Bangor airport. It was 3 years since I had seen him. He hadn't changed except for the odd grey hair in his black beard. We weren't going to stay in his cabin in Patten as it was too cold and he had to turn off the water and drain the system in case the pipes burst. Mark said we could stay in his ranch house (bungalow) which was 50 miles west of Bangor. The area we were going to hunt in was between Orono (where the old town Canadian canoe comes from) and Grand Lake stream to Machias in Down East Maine. It hadn't snowed in a few days but there was still about 4" of old snow on the ground. Maybe it would be enough to find a Bobcat print?

It was Monday 2nd January so Mark called me for breakfast: scrambled eggs, rashers and coffee. I went outside and it felt like 20°F below freezing. It was 6a.m. and pitch black outside. Mark turned on the engine of the Chevy pick-up. We had to scrape the frost off the windscreen and sweep out the snow, which had lodged in the flatbed of the truck.

The dogs we would use were the same dogs we had used on previous occasions for hunting bear. There were two novices but Gus who was Mark's top dog was still going to be the leader of the pack. The dogs would have tracking collars but unlike bear hunting a strike dog would not be put on top of the cab. At 15mph and at 20° below, I'd imagine that a polar bear would have problems dealing with the wind factor.

We arrived at the hunting area when it was still dark. Mark turned on the C.B. to let logging truck drivers know that we were entering the area. Logging trucks have the right of way so it is important that everybody knows that there is traffic in the most isolated of areas. There was a spotlight mounted to the side of the cab on the passenger side. The light was pointed downward and towards the verge of the gravel road that was now covered in packed snow. The road was like a skating rink in some places but we took our time. Snowploughs had left a three to four-foot high bank of snow on each side of the road. Any animal, which crossed the road during the night or early morning, would have left their prints in the snow. My job was to keep an eye out for tracks, which looked like a bobcat.

I find it easy to track deer or foxes through wet earth or boggy soil in Ireland. Tracking animals in snow is a lot more difficult than it seems. Deer tracks are especially difficult because if the snow is deep it may be difficult to ascertain in what direction the animal is travelling. At one stage I thought that I saw cat tracks. Mark got out and examined them. Mark explained that bobcat prints are slightly broader and that there may be fur marks in between the pads. The Coyote does not retract his claws unlike the Bobcat.

We kept driving until dawn but all we found were Coyote and deer prints. At one stage a solitary coyote crossed the road in front of the truck. Soon afterwards the spotlight picked out three sets of eyes which belonged to a pack of coyotes hunting in a small pine copse. As soon as the truck stopped they bolted into the darkness. We didn't spot any deer as they were probably lying up in the deer yards for shelter and food.

Dawn soon broke to reveal a winter wonderland. Every opening amongst the trees had a crystal covering of snow, all the streams were frozen over as well as every lake and pond. The white pyramid of snow in the frozen ice revealed beaver lodges. The frost glistened in an azure glow on the old logging trails. There was no breeze and the sky was cloudless. When we stepped outside and turned off the engine there was nothing to be heard except the sound of silence. All the waterfowl had left for the warmer areas

TO HUNT, SHOOT AND STALK

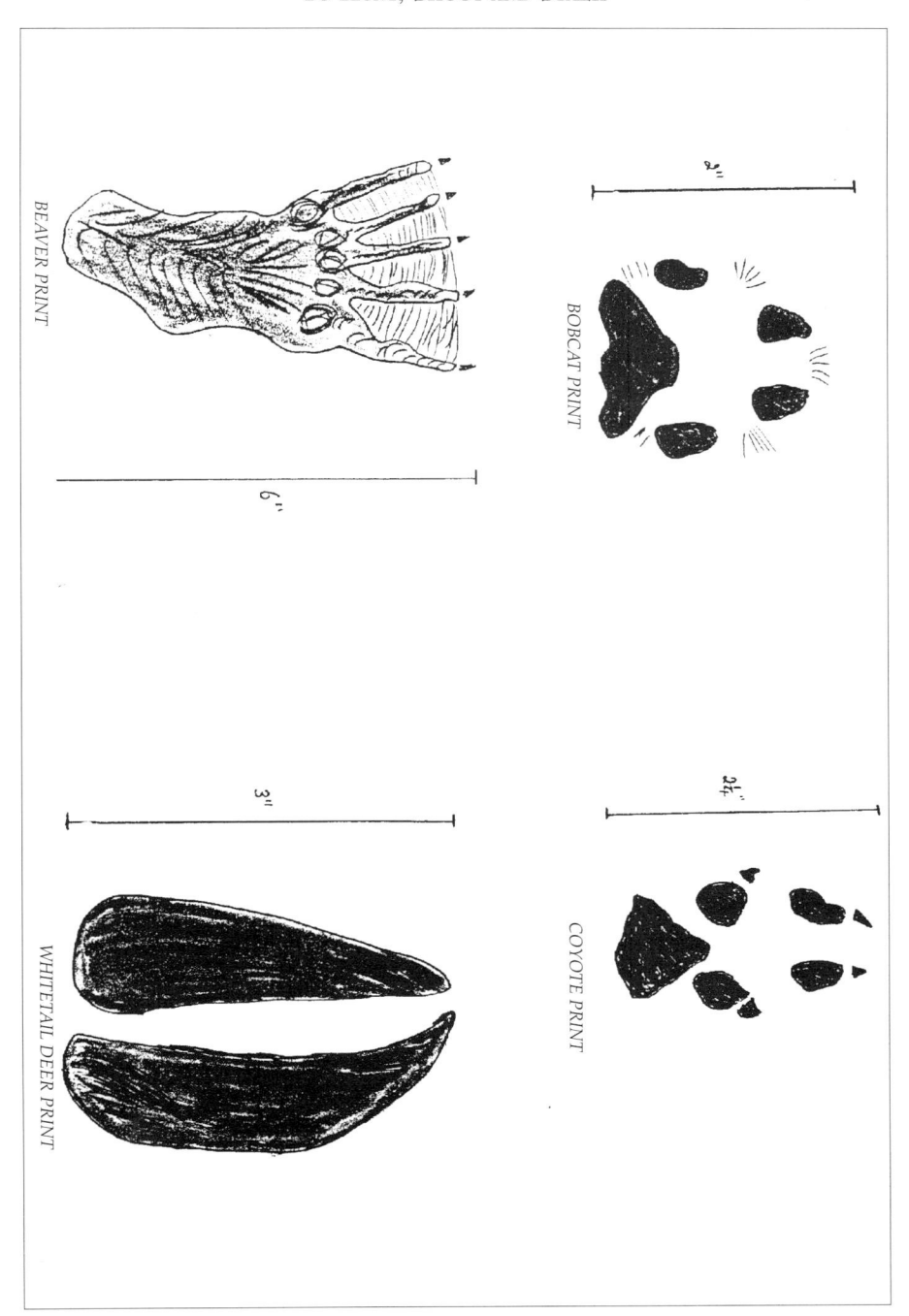

BEAVER PRINT
6"

BOBCAT PRINT
2"

WHITETAIL DEER PRINT
3"

COYOTE PRINT
2¼"

like Chesapeake Bay and the Mississippi basin.

Mark had scouted the area the previous week and marked the crossing point of a cat with surveyor's tape. He decided to go to this location to see if there were any fresh prints. It hadn't snowed in four days so the snow was crusted on top, which made it unsuitable for sinking paws. The best time to hunt cat is after a fall of fresh snow. It makes it more difficult for the bobcat's prey to move in these conditions but it also means that the cat moves slowly and does not travel as far. If it is difficult for the four-legged species to travel in deep fresh snow you can imagine how hard it is for the two-legged type. If the snow was very deep and fresh we would have to use the old Indian method and wear snow-shoes. I was hoping that we would be using a snowmobile but Mark's had been vandalised and was presently in the repair shop.

We found the surveyor's tape four feet inside the mound of snow at the side of the road. Mark pointed to the old track but it was quite obvious that nothing had travelled that trail lately. Ten miles further on we turned down an old logging road where there were no tyre tracks to be seen. As we passed over a small frozen stream we saw a set of tracks in the dusting of snow which had lodged on top of the ice.

They were bobcat prints, probably a big old tom but they weren't fresh. Since our prospects didn't look too good so far we decided to let out Gus to 'cold-trail' the cat. An experienced hound will know after following an old trail if it will lead to an animal who may have rested up in the area. The cats will often lie out in the sun in the morning if they have been hunting all night. Gus followed the trail for about twenty minutes but it just died out.

We cold trailed like this a number of times but to no avail. Crusty old snow can make a dog's paw raw and ice can cut the pads. After two hours we left for home. The weather forecast was for snow that night. The temperature was rising and clouds were coming in from the west. If it snowed tonight conditions would be ideal in the morning.

The study in Mark's house was full of beautifully mountained specimens. He had a noble twelve point buck and a shoulder mount of a large black bear. He had some classic bobcat rugs and an impressive full mounted tom on a large piece of driftwood. Mark's pride and joy was the mountain lion, which he got in Montana the previous January. It took him about five days to drive from Maine to the Rocky Mountains. He drove in the Chevy and brought along his own dogs for the hunt. They had not hunted lion before but they excelled themselves. They met three lions in five days and Mark took one large tom with a .22 magnum rifle. The cougars or mountain lions look quite large but they may weigh only 120-140 lbs.

At 5.30 a.m. the following morning the first snowflakes began to fall. We were disappointed because we had hoped to have a good covering at this stage. It may be too late for a night cat to leave his tracks in the snow. The weather forecast at 6 a.m. said that there was going to be a blizzard and not to travel unless absolutely necessary. After 3,000 miles a blizzard was not going to stop me so we set off.

Route 95 North goes all the way to Canada. Route 95 South will take you to the Florida Keys. We were heading North and the snowflakes were dazzling us in the headlights of the truck. The odd car was sliding into the hard shoulder and the orange flashing lights of the snowploughs could be seen in the distance. We headed East on Route 2 and then took Stud Mill Road to enter the wilderness.

We switched on the spotlight but it was impossible to find any tracks. Even if there were tracks they would have been filled up instantly as the flakes were tumbling down so fast.

At daybreak it was still snowing hard and it certainly looked as though the blizzard would last for the day. We saw no animal at all and even though we checked at the same places where we had been yesterday there was no sign of fresh tracks. Any sensible cat would be in his den with such conditions.

After much deliberation we said that we would take a chance and drive down an unused logging trail. The trail was covered in about six to ten inches of snow. It looked perfectly safe but we knew precious little of what was underneath.

During the November deer season the road was constantly driven by out of state hunters in their 4x4's. November had been wet and the roads had been badly rutted. The ruts had filled with water to a depth of six to twelve inches and had frozen solid over the last few weeks. Suddenly the wheels began to spin and we slipped into a small gully at the side. Try as he might Mark could not get out of this predicament.

I got out and tried to shove the two tonnes of metal but it was going nowhere. We got a pair of spades and began to shovel away the fresh powered snow, only to reveal a complete trail of solid ice. We took out the manual winch and connected one end to the front axle and the other end to the nearest suitable tree. As Mark applied the pressure the tree groaned and bent over. Twice more we did this but always with the same results.

The storm was raging now and we could hardly make out each other's face through the swirling snow. We crawled in under the chassis and began to break the ice with hammers and crowbars. Mark got into the cab and slipped the Chevy into gear. The wheels gradually wore away the crushed ice and made contact with the earth. He put it into a low forward pulling gear and after what seemed an age the Chevy pulled itself out and was now resting on level ground. We said that we would head back for home as the weather was constantly deteriorating. We edged slowly forward looking for a suitable place to turn about. We saw what looked like a perfect place and prayed that there was no hidden obstacle underneath. Everything worked out ok. but we still had to drive back through the area where we got stuck. Mark kept the wheels straight and drove at about 20 m.p.h. following a slightly different line to earlier on. Allelulia! We were safely through and headed back for civilization.

When you go hunting or travelling into the Maine back-woods you have to be always prepared. We had a C.B. on board and a cellular phone. If we went into unknown territory or knew that we were going to separate we would carry Marine Radios. There was two and a half days supply of petrol in the tank and we had two flasks of coffee, soft drinks and sandwiches. We could sleep with the dogs in the cab if things came to their worst.

Third day lucky! It stopped snowing at 1 a.m. that night so it looked like providing ideal conditions for a proper bobcat hunt. We loaded the dogs into the truck as well as guns, cartridges, extra pairs of socks and food. The socks wouldn't be used till the end of the day as there would be many instances of wet feet from snow covered potholes. We would hunt in the general area of the previous days but a little further to the east. The main roads had been totally cleared by the snowploughs so we made good time.

Soon after 8 a.m. Mark spotted cat tracks. They had to be fresh and sure enough Mark said that it was a big Tom. Judging by the depth of the print he reckoned the cat weighed about 40 lbs. The trail led towards a boulder field. This was a large area of rocks and boulders, which was a remnant of the Ice Age. Cats like to den in these areas, as there are plenty of small caves and suitable sunning areas. Mark had one of his dogs go to ground here last year and it was two and a half days before he got him out. Eventually Mark had to be lowered on a rope in order to reach his dog.

Mark chose two of the four dogs who hopefully would not follow the cat to ground. He certainly did not want a repeat of last year's episode. The dogs began to give tongue, which indicated that the Tom was just ahead of them. We were on the road at the base of a hill and in the still morning air we could hear everything. The barking stopped but then the sounds kept coming back from one specific area. The cat had gone to ground. Mark called up the dogs immediately and after ten minutes they returned. It was easy to see the relief in his face even though he was disappointed that we didn't get the Tom.

We stopped for lunch and tried to review our next plan of action. It was 11 a.m. and the sun was shining brightly with just a few clouds in the sky. Mark's strategy was to drive over the next hill and down to a valley where there were small silver-fir copses and a frozen creek running through it.

As we reached the brow of the hill I noticed tracks on a small embankment of snow. Mark double checked them and said that it was a pair of cats hunting together – a male and a female. He knew where they led so he decided to drive down the road for six hundred yards and to look for where they might cross again. Sure enough the same pair of tracks was located. There was no snow in the paw marks so they had to be fresh. Mark took all the dogs into the forest and told me to wait on the road as the cats would more than likely backtrail in order to confuse the dogs.

I took the Franchi out of the cab and loaded it with the three no. 4 copper plated 2-inch magnum shells. The copper plating is to give more penetration and to hold the lead pellet in one solid piece. Similar cartridges were used for shooting wild turkey, which may weigh up to 22 lbs. I had my balaclava with me so I pulled down the mask and stood with my back to a tree. The dogs began howling immediately so I knew that we were in business. I could see the dogs at times but even though I peered in front to see the cats I never even saw a shadow of them. Mark roared back that he had found the carcass of a deer. Apparently they had been feeding on it before they were disturbed.

The barking changed direction just as the dogs and phantom cats seemed to be coming my way. The cats did a turnabout and were heading downhill towards the distant creek. The sound of the dogs became fainter but I was certain that they were still trailing. Mark ran up to me with sweat streaming down his face. He knew the line the cats were taking and if we were lucky we should be able to head them off when they tried to cross the next road.

We ran back to the truck and proceeded to a wooden bridge, which crossed the creek. When I stepped out I could hear the dogs on the right bank of the creek but I couldn't catch a glance of them. At 250 yards range the dogs barked loudly and I was prepared to see a cat bolt out of the silver firs at any moment.

No cat appeared from anywhere along the gravel road but the barking began again 150 yards in front of me near a little bend in the stream . The sounds kept coming from the one spot. The dogs must have had a cat at bay or treed. I stumbled through the powdered snow as I inched my way through the thick copse. The howls were only 25 yards away so I was ready for action. As I broke from cover I saw two dogs barking at the base of a tall pine tree in the middle of the frozen water. I edged my way slowly forward but still I couldn't see the cat. The dogs were convinced that the cat was in the tree but they were wrong! There was a blowdown resting against the top of the pine. Apparently the cat had gone up the tree but had used one of its nine lives to go down the other side and escape unknown to the dogs. I still hadn't seen sight or sound of a bobcat.

Suddenly the other dogs began barking 250 yards to my right on the side of a small hill. Mark was over there and he shouted at me that he had just seen the cat go into a copse of firs. The firs were about 4 feet high on average but very thickly planted. When I got up to where Mark was I heard something bolt from behind. I swung around but it was only a white-tailed doe. We thought that the dogs were on a false trail when they entered the copse again but out bolted a lovely spotted bob. I was about to fire but Mark said not to as the dogs were too close at hand. I was inclined to argue the point with him as I was well used to shooting foxes in Ireland with a terrier close behind.

The cat ran into the centre of the cover and I knew that the dogs had him or her at bay. It was too thick to work a shotgun with a 28" barrel. To get to where the cat was I would have to crawl and if snow got into the barrel the consequences could be deadly. Mark took out his 1920 Colt Woodsman .22 handgun. I had never hunted with a handgun but I had completed a proficiency course in Boston using many types of handguns. If I could get a shot at close range I wouldn't do as much damage to the pelt as a shotgun would.

I crept through the trees on all fours with the barrel of the pistol held high above the snow. Ten feet in front I saw the bobcat and fired a shot behind the shoulder. It was a she cat weighing 28 lbs. She had beautiful spots on her pelt like a small leopard. Unlike a leopard her tail was only about 3' long. Her mate, the Tom escaped and we never caught sight or sound of him again. It was now 4 p.m., the clouds had rolled in and the light was beginning to fade. We gathered up the dogs and began the long journey back to base.

CHAPTER FIFTEEN

Red Deer Stalking in Scotland

The Red Deer (Cervus Elaphus) or the Fia Rua as it is called in Irish, is native to North America, Southern Canada, Europe and North Africa. It was introduced by the early settlers to New Zealand and Australia for hunting purposes. In North America the red deer is called the Waipiti. Red deer roamed over most of Ireland but due to de-afforestation and hunting pressure, they are found now in parts of Kerry, Wicklow, Donegal and Meath. The red deer came under severe pressure in Ireland during the Great Famine 'An Gorta' of 1845 to 1847. The last red deer on the Galtee Mountains was supposed to have been killed during this period. Red deer shooting is regulated carefully in Ireland and shooting is basically only allowed in County Wicklow. The season for stags runs from 1st September to the end of February. The females or hinds can be shot from 1st November to the 31st January – however, an extension may come into this season sometimes. Red deer are experiencing problems in Wicklow due to interbreeding with the Sika deer. The hybrid offspring are jeopardising the pure red deer population. Red deer are thriving in the natural oak forests of Killarney which is now a National Park where no hunting is allowed.

Red deer in Ireland and Scotland once lived solely in deciduous forests but due to the habitat destruction, they now live on some open mountains and moorland. They also inhabit pine forests which border mountain areas. They are grazers and browsers; stripping the bark from young trees to get the minerals which they need. Ferns, heather fungi and lichens will also be eaten.

The russet brown colour of the hide gives the deer its name. They may live for twelve to fifteen years. The mating season or rut takes place from September to November. During this time, the stag grows a thick mane on his neck. The neck also swells during the rut to give him a more impressive appearance. A one year old stag will have prong-like antlers like horns. New points are added every year and a mature stag may have up to sixteen points. A twelve point animal is called a royal stag. Stags live in bachelor groups or herds outside of the mating season. Females may live in herds numbering from five hundred plus animals. During the rut, however, the dominant stags set up their own harems by bellowing loudly to attract hinds and to repel other males. The calves are born around May and have a white speckled coat. Red deer never have white spots on their hide at any other stage of their lives. Like the white-tail deer, the red deer will raise its tail to expose a cream-coloured rump to warn the other members of the herd of any impending danger. Frightened deer may exit an area at up to 60 km per hour (38 m per hour).

Stalking is the main method of hunting red deer. Stalking means finding the objective of your hunt, approaching it with stealth and then taking the shot when the target is within range. Still-hunting is a term which Americans use. You do not see the object of the hunt so you move forward quietly and stop for a few minutes in order to hear the sound of moving animals or else to spot them doing so. A hunter sees the deer before he or she begins the stalk. Jumping or driving deer entails searching thick brush and woodland with the off chance of pushing the animal out into the open.

The best place to stalk deer is on open moorland or heather covered mountains. The Highlands of Scotland provide such places and it was there that I went to stalk red deer in the early 1990's. At that time I used a .22/250 B.S.A. rifle for hunting deer in Ireland. The minimum calibre for shooting red deer in Scotland was .270. At that time it was illegal to possess a .270 in Ireland.

Through an advertisement in an Irish shooting magazine, I made arrangements to hunt in the Highlands North of Pitlochry. The nearest city in Scotland to Pitlochry is Perth. The best time to stalk was in late September or October, but I could only go at the end of August. It was really too early for the rut but with some effort I might get a nice stag. There was no chance of a Royal as these are protected for breeding purposes. An eight pointer would be sufficient as far as I was concerned.

I travelled by car to Larne in Northern Ireland and across to Stranraer in Scotland by ferry. The journey up to Glasgow was through the poet Robert Burn's country, and past the Mull of Kintyre, made famous by the Paul McCartney song. After that it was on the motorways to Perth, and then on to Pitlochry, past ancient Scottish castles and famous salmon rivers like the Tay. One road-sign pointed towards the town of Dunkeld. Prior to this, the only Dunkeld I knew was an attractor trout fly. I made my way to the Bed and Breakfast where I was to stay for the next two nights. It was situated on a private farm about two miles from the town of Pitlochry. I wasn't due to go stalking till the following day so I decided to explore Pitlochry for the afternoon.

There was a hydro-electric station there which was open to the public. The station is situated where Lough Faskally enters the river Tay. The Atlantic salmon have to pass through a fish ladder in order to circumnavigate the dam and enter the lough. Part of the ladder consisted of glass tanks through which the fish could be observed making their upward migration. There had been heavy rain in the highlands and the water was stained. Leaves and other small particles of debris passed by the salmon but they seemed undeterred.

'Scotch' is made in Scotland and each large town seems to have its own distillery and Pitlochry is no exception. There was a small distillery which provided guided tours for visitors. The guide explained how the copper pots worked and how the alcohol made its way through the coiled cooling pipe. Barley from different areas of Scotland is malted and then put into oak casks where it is bonded and allowed to mature. The casks help to add colour and taste to the whiskey. At the end of the tour, each visitor is given a chance to try a shot-glass of the different blends. A very 'warming' experience I must say! That night I met some American tourists who were staying in the Bed and Breakfast, so we decided to go to the theatre. I had to be at the estate at 9.00 a.m. so I wasn't worried about sleeping it out. In Ireland or America, I was familiar with rising well before dawn.

The pheasants on the driveway into the estate were the only things that hindered my progress from Pitlochry. Driven shoots took place on the estate from October and these birds were part of this year's crop. The gamekeeper was standing beside a long-wheel-base Landrover when I entered the courtyard. He was dressed in tweeds and wearing a Sherlock Holmes stalking hat. His tie was immaculately tied about his cotton shirt. We shook hands and I began to ask him one hundred questions.

Richard was his name and he seemed surprised when I told him that I had no gun. I explained the Irish situation to him and soon enough I had a Bruno .270 in my hands. We tested it out at one hundred and fifty yards and when we were both satisfied, we decided to commence our stalk. There was no mist on the mountains and there was no breeze. Visibility was excellent and the weather was cool enough for hill climbing. We would have had to abandon our hunt if the mountains were shrouded in mist or clouds. The bullets we were using were Winchester 130 grain silver tipped. The nosler partition would guarantee controlled expansion and humane killing power. A red deer stag can weigh from one hundred and fifty up to seven hundred pounds; or four hundred pounds on average.

The estate farm bordered ten thousand acres of open mountain and heather. We had to walk five hundred yards through a pine forest before we reached the open hill. I could see the tracks of deer going through the pines but there were no deer there at the moment. Richard climbed over a dry stone wall which ran along the edge of the forest and I followed behind. As I stood on top of the five foot wall, I saw a hill which was five hundred feet high about one-quarter of a mile away. Standing on the side of the hill was a herd of approximately five hundred reds. They were all hinds and I didn't see one antler amongst them. They eyed us warily for two minutes and then took off over the brow of the hill.

Richard's plan of action was to follow the stone wall for about a mile as it would provide cover for our stalk. The wall turned at right angles and as we came around the corner, a startled roe buck stood looking at us. He was safe today so he jumped the wall and disappeared into the pines. The gamekeeper had hoped that we might come across a stag but there was none to be seen. Richard used his telescope to glass the area but to no avail. He decided to go back to the farmyard and get the Landrover. We would drive a few miles into the mountains and then climb to higher ground. Midges are an annoyance to red deer at this time of the year and many herds go to the tops of the hills where the cool breezes keep the insects at bay.

We parked the jeep at a wooden cabin. There are many similar cabins or huts scattered throughout the Highlands. They are used by hill climbers and shepherds. We sat down at the wooden table and bench to have our lunch. There was an old 'visitors book' lying on the table and as I glanced through it I saw an inscription from an Australian hiker. There were no climbers to be seen on the hills today. The deer, if there were any, would not be disturbed before we approached.

After lunch we tried a gully where Richard had seen two nice stags the day before – today however the area was vacant except for a small herd of roe deer. There are no roe deer in Ireland and it was interesting just to study them. They were one hundred and fifty yards away and provided a nice shot for a roe deer hunter.

We began to climb a hill which was about one thousand feet high. It was extremely steep and at times I had to hold onto the purple heather and pull myself upwards. The ground was dry underneath but I would imagine that it would be very slippery in wet weather. The view from the top provided a panorama. Visibility was at least ten miles and I could see lakes, rivers and mountains in every direction. Balmoral was only twenty miles due North. Richard called me and pointed to a stag with a lop-sided antler which had been damaged in a sparring match. It was important that such an animal should be culled, so we decided to initiate our stalk. He was at the bottom of a valley and moving slowly along the dividing fence between us and the next estate. He hadn't seen us but he was moving up the valley all the time. He was about seven hundred yards away so we decided to move slowly through the thick heather and to keep a low profile. There was a small turf embankment about two hundred and fifty yards down below us. We would get behind it and try to get within range.

Our descent went according to plan until there was a loud 'craak-craak' as a pack of grouse flushed from the heather. They flew forward, descended to the valley and glided up the far side and out of sight. This is one of the main problems encountered when stalking in Scotland. The grouse may often alert the deer to the fact that there is a stalker in the area. However, they did not spook our stag. I personally thought that it was great to see so many grouse on the mountain. In Ireland they are becoming a rare commodity. Richard explained that the grouse moors are further away from the stalking areas. However, the birds will take nature's course and breed in other areas if they have suitable habitat and a lack of predators. There were no sheep to be seen in this area. They are not allowed in stalking sections and I also noticed that there was no sign of heather burning or soil erosion due to over-grazing. Whatever breeze was there today, it was blowing into our faces. The deer couldn't smell us but for some particular reason, he began to move swiftly and soon was disappearing over a high ridge which was about a half mile away. There was no point in following him now as it would take too long to get to the top. We saw two other sets of antlers go over the ridge in the same location. Maybe this was why our chosen animal departed the scene.

We glassed the hills again and about one mile to the east I spotted a 'forest' of antlers. On top of the hill there was a bachelor herd of fifty stags just lying down in the heather. My heart almost stopped with excitement as I was sure that we would surely get one even though it would entail a difficult climb. The deer did not have to worry.

They were on the next estate and we couldn't approach them. There was a low wire fence dividing our estate from the opposite one. Stalkers were allowed to take a deer to one hundred and fifty yards of the far side but no more. We sat down to take in the scenery before moving on to a corry where Richard said that we had a good chance of getting an animal. We were two thousand to three thousand feet above sea level and the landscape was challenging but the spectacular scenery made it all worthwhile. Richard explained that during the Falklands War, the R.A.F. pilots used make low level practise runs along the side of the hill where we were now sitting. He was often able to look down into their cockpits when he was checking the deer. Two miles below us was a mountain lake or lough as they are called in Scotland. There was a fisherman's hut at the side and it was a haven for the fly fishermen who sought wild brownies. The trout may be small at these attitudes but they are good fighters and as wild as you can get. I had my fishing rods in the car and if we got a stag I hoped to catch a Scottish salmon or maybe a sea trout.

Corries were the starting points for glaciers during the last ice age. The snow and ice built up in the three sided hollow and finally a glacier moved out slowly to carve a u-shaped valley. After the ice melted a lake was left in the deep hollow. Some hollows had no lakes similar to the one which we were creeping towards. We crawled through the heather and peered down from one of the steep sides. It was an ideal place for an ambush but today it was devoid of any deer. I thought I saw a roe deer on the far side but on closer examination it turned out to be a large mountain hare. It was now 12.30 p.m. so we headed back towards the pine forest. There were plenty of deer droppings and tracks but the deer must have been deep in the undergrowth, as the sun was high in the sky, and it was quite hot. We decided to abandon our hunt till the evening when the air would be cooler and animals more active. I decided to go back to Pitlochry to get some lunch and then to take a short nap.

I got a phone call from the gamekeeper at 5.00 p.m. to hurry out to the estate. A herd of deer had moved out of the pines and were grazing in the neighbouring field. I changed into my hunting apparel and entered the courtyard where the engine of the landrover was ticking over. Richard had a driver ready so I jumped into the back. Ten minutes later we stopped at a clearing in the middle of the forest. The field was about two hundred yards away. There was no breeze so we didn't have to worry about the deer scenting us. We moved cautiously though a fire-break and soon we were at the stone wall which bordered the field. There was no sign of the deer but Richard explained that the field dipped into a hollow beyond a rocky outcrop which was seventy-five yards beyond the wall.

The driver remained back at the jeep while Richard and I crawled towards the outcrop. Three minutes later we were behind a large boulder which blocked our view. We peered over it and one hundred and twenty-five yards below us we spotted the herd of fourteen hinds with the stag in the middle. Richard handed me the .270 Brno and I edged to the right hand side of the boulder where I got a good rest on a clump of grasses. The stag was plainly visible but the hinds were moving around him. Twice I had the cross hairs on his neck but each time the hinds crossed in front or beside him. For some reason or other, the deer became very alert and began to move off. I followed the stag's progress with the scope but dared not fire. Suddenly they stopped and there was a gap on either side of the stag. The cross hairs were on the base of his neck so I squeezed the trigger slowly. He dropped on the spot and we waited for two minutes before we approached. The hinds had jumped the wall at this stage and were hiding deep in the forest.

The stag was in great condition and the shot had entered the base of the neck. Richard and I shook hands as the driver appeared from the top of the outcrop. From where we were standing, it was easy to see why the deer did not detect us.

Hunting magazines show pictures of ponies or garrons carrying home the trophy. This method is seldom used nowadays as I soon learned. Richard told the driver to go back to the farm and soon afterwards we were loading the deer on the front of an A.T.V. Back at the larder Richard hung up the deer and washed the chest cavity. He would boil the head as I would take just the skull and antlers home. Generally speaking the carcass is kept by the estate who sell it on to game dealers.

A tributary of the Tay flowed through the estate so Richard invited me to go salmon fishing the following morning. He would have the head ready by 2.00 p.m. so it would be a good way of passing the time. He explained to me how to get to the good lies where he had seen salmon the previous day.

At 9.00 a.m. I was on a bridge overlooking the river. I saw where the salmon pool was so I set off with a small fly rod with a 'thunder and lightning' salmon fly. I could hear thunder on the hills and it had been raining heavily during the night. The river was beginning to rise and debris was floating down. Soon it was in full spate and the fishing was finished. I turned to go back to the bridge and there in the middle of a kale field was a fine roe buck – maybe he was of gold medal quality. Hopefully I would return to the Highlands and hunt roe deer in the near future.

CHAPTER SIXTEEN

Clay Pigeon Shooting
– The Flapper Shoot

Clay pigeon shooting is an ideal way of practising during the close season. It helps the hunter to improve his accuracy and it is also a very suitable method for instructing newcomers to the techniques of shooting with shotguns. Youngsters can be taught the basics of firearms. Most important of all is that the safety aspect of guns can be explained in a controlled environment.

The Irish Clay Pigeon Association (I.C.P.S.A.) deals with registered or formal shoots where participants are graded and where strict guidelines with regards to procedure are enforced. Contestants are chosen from I.C.P.S.A. registered shoots to pick individuals and teams for national and international competitions. I do not propose to deal with the registered shoot but rather the 'Flapper' or unregistered shoot. The flapper shoot is generally organised by a local gun club and is open to all shooters. Generally a club organises such a shoot to raise funds in order to release pheasants or mallard. Sometimes a shoot may be organised to raise funds for a charitable reason.

The Suir Valley and District Gun Club ran a clay pigeon shoot in 1999 to provide funds for F.H.I.S.T. (Funded Housing Initiative in South Tipperary). Many other clubs in the South Tipperary Regional Game Council supported the event and one thousand, three hundred and sixty pounds was raised.

Flapper shoots take a lot of hard work and preparation and sometimes a bit of luck if they are to be successful. The first thing is to decide on is a suitable date – don't pick a day on which there is an important local or national G.A.A. match. The secretary should apply two weeks in advance of the chosen date for N.A.R.G.C. insurance. The fee is ten pounds and it is the best value for money of any form of insurance. The N.A.R.G.C. also supplies safety posters for shoots and the Regional Safety Officer will attend on the day. Clubs should have their own safety officer who should be well educated or experienced in all forms of gun safety. Everybody should wear proper ear-protection. I have shot clay pigeons in an American Gun Club and eye-protection was mandatory as well as ear plugs or muffs.

The shoot can be advertised in the local paper, in shooting magazines or fliers can be sent to local gun club secretaries. Sponsorship has to be sought and also a suitable venue which is not too far off the main road. Many competitors have problems finding the actual venue due to the lack of visible directions. There is no point in putting up a sign if it is so low that it is covered by grass or so high up in a tree that a passing motorist never sees it.

The springs on manual traps should be checked and spare springs should be available on the day. The trappers should be familiar with the traps and they should be relieved regularly – accidents happen when people get tired. It is advisable to have a first aid kit available in case of mishaps. Alternatively the trapper may change with the person marking the card. The most important thing is to provide proper and adequate protection for the trapper. Round bales, square bales, sheets of M.D.F., corrugated iron or 3 mm steel are often used on their own or in different combinations.

I once saw a trap house built of square bales of barley-straw piled on top of each other. It was decided to fire a No. 7 cartridge into the bales at approximately fifteen paces. A sheet of newspaper was suspended on the trapper's side of the bales. After the shot we examined the paper and saw one hole where a pellet had passed through the place where the bales were joined together. One pellet hitting a human in the spine could cause terrible human suffering. We doubled up the bales, put a couple of sheets of M.D.F. in front and did the test again. This time no pellet passed through. The traps or stands should be roped off from observers – only the person shooting should be allowed inside.

The trap set-up at a flapper shoot is generally called 'sporting', that is, the action of the clay pigeon resembles an actual game bird or animal. The springing teal trap is meant to resemble a teal rising from a pond. A sporting gun generally has a twenty-eight inch barrel and is lighter than a trap gun which may measure thirty, thirty-one or thirty-two inches.

The club committee should decide how many traps they are going to use and whether there will be a high gun prize for the best competitor over all the various traps. Generally there will be ten clays or birds. They are generally given in four singles and three doubles – however, the shoot will run faster if the clays are thrown in doubles and more profit will be generated at the end of the day. Some clubs allow only 'one man – one prize'. This prevents the professional clay shooter from winning all the prizes and is basically a type of handicap. Disputes should go to a special committee which may include the secretary, chairperson and one outsider.

I will deal with a number of different sporting disciplines and give some useful directions with regard to layout, clays, chokes, shot size and techniques for 'dusting' the clays. The hints may not be written in stone as each club will have its own individual way of organising events.

Springing Teal: The shooter generally is ten to fifteen paces away from the trap. The clays may be all black or all blaze. They may be given as four singles and three doubles or all doubles. Full and three-quarter chokes are generally the best with No. 8 and 7½ cartridges. The gun may be held on the shoulder or mounted as the bird is called. The single bird moves faster than a double, so shoot it as you pass it out. When shooting doubles, shoot the slower bird first before it begins to drop and then fire under the second bird if it has begun to drop.

Cock and Hen: The shooter stands beside the trap. Five doubles are thrown consisting of a blaze and black clay. The blaze clay must always be shot first. The trapper can vary the way the clays travel by putting the blaze clay on top or underneath and doing so in any pattern – however the clays should be placed on the same area of the trap each time. The best way of having fairly consistent clays is by marking the trap with a heavy black marker. A shooter often has to compete against the trapper as well as other competitors. Quarter and half chokes are suitable with No. 7½ and No. 8 cartridges. The best technique is to take the blaze clay as fast as you can. The gun may be held at the shoulder or mounted with the bird.

High Pheasant: The trap is generally twenty feet behind the shooter. It may be on a hill or a high trailer. Mattie Kennedy (R.I.P.) was a famous Cattle Transporter in South Tipperary and he always provided his truck for our clay shoots. It was driven into place and the trap was mounted on a railway sleeper on top of the trailer section. The clays are coming from behind the shooter so the trapper does not need protection. The clays may be given in four singles and three doubles or all doubles. Skeet and one-quarter chokes are best with No. 8 shot. The clays, depending on the layout, will pass about fifteen to thirty yards over the shooter's head. The trap will be behind so you will often hear the clays before you see them. Listen also to the sound of the trap being released, keep your head back and your gun up. I find that if you wear a peaked cap you have less time to observe the targets. However, many people shoot better than I do and they keep their caps on. Shoot under the clays as they are dropping all the time. The clays are generally black – remember that you will be looking at the clay from underneath.

Crossing Pigeon: The trap may be twenty yards to either the right or the left of the shooter. The clays will pass about ten yards out in front. They may be given in singles or doubles and the speed will depend on how tight the spring on the trap is. Black or blaze clays may be used. The best choke is skeet or one-quarter, but this can vary with the trap layout. No. 8 and No. 7 cartridges are best. Follow through and give a good lead to the first bird and then take the second as soon as you can. The second bird will be slowing down but it may also be disappearing behind some distant obstacle like a tree. Most shooters consider the crossing pigeon to be the most difficult target. It is a great way of dividing up competitors who may have had high scores on other traps. Everybody finds it difficult to put up a possible, that is, one hundred ex one hundred on this particular trap. There will be a lot of unbroken clays to be picked up in this area when the day is over.

Breaking Snipe: The layout is similar to the cock and hen and the shooter is standing beside the trap. The clays exit the trap at about four feet from the ground and going extremely fast. The clays can be thrown in six singles and two doubles or all doubles. The clays may be black or blaze but not mixed. The most suitable chokes to use are one-quarter and three-quarters with No. 8 and 9's in the right barrel, and No. 7's in the left. The competitor may stand with the gun to the shoulder or mount the gun with the bird. Shoot fast firing at the slowest bird first before it has a chance to hit the ground.

Bolting Rabbit: This trap is a great crowd-puller and great fun also. The only draw-back is that you can only fire singles. The clays are generally blaze and are flatter and heavier compared to the normal clay. The trap is of a different design because the clay is fired onto the ground and not over. The trap is set up about sixteen paces from the stand; the clay is first fired onto an eight foot strip of carpet which is hidden from the shooter; this causes the clay to bounce and it also stops it from shattering when it first strikes the ground. The rabbit is concealed from view by bales of straw with a seven to nine foot gap in between. The clay is shot at as it is passing across this point. The 'rabbit' moves so fast that the competitor gets only one shot. Call and shoot using skeet chokes with No. 8 or No. 9 cartridges. Sometimes the rabbit will roll along and at times it will bounce about a foot into the air. The bolting- rabbit can become very addictive as you strive to get ten ex ten. The competitor may hold his or her gun to the shoulder and point at a particular spot where he or she finds that most of the clays can be intercepted.

Down-The-Line (D.T.L.): The D.T.L. trap may comprise of ten, fifteen or twenty-five single blaze clays. The trap is concealed in a trap-house the top of which should be three feet above ground level. The house may be a permanent fixture made of concrete blocks or 3 mm steel. Five competitors take part, the stands are sixteen paces from the trap and about three to five feet apart. At a ten bird D.T.L. the shooter fires at two clays on each stand, three at the fifteen D.T.L. and five at the twenty-five bird. A first shot 'kill' gets a score of ten whereas a second shot kill gets five points. The trap may be automatic or manual – D.T.L. entails a lot of fast targets so it is tiring for the trapper. Trap houses can also be hot and humid during fine weather. If an automatic trap is being used, a 'button-person' will be needed as well as a marker. The 'button' releases the trap arm. Semi-automatic traps have to be loaded each time by a trapper.

The stands or pegs are numbered one to five going from left to right. The shooter always has the gun mounted to his shoulder. If you are a right handed shooter, have your left foot forward and vice versa. Full and three-quarter chokes are the most suitable with No. 7 or No. 8 cartridges. Remember that on the professional shooting circuit, the trap gun is heavier than the sporting gun and has a higher or an adjustable stock. There are also two beads on the rib of the professional trap – shot gun.

If you are standing at peg No. 1 aim at point A on the trap house, see diagram. This gives you the tightest angle and the most time. When you call 'pull', follow the clay, cover it and fire. When standing at peg No. 2 aim at point B, call and fire in the same manner. Follow the same procedure for pegs 3, 4 and 5. Peg No.3 is the easiest to fire from as the clay is basically going straight away from you. As you go to the left or right of this peg, the rate of difficulty increases. If the angle of delivery is very wide at pegs 1 and 5, you may have to lead the clay by an appropriate amount. If in doubt, ask an expert or go to a professional shooting coach. Again a trapper can increase the difficulty of the target by positioning it on different places on the trap.

Double-barrel shotguns should only be closed on the D.T.L. stand when you are about to fire. If you are moving from stand number five to stand number one, unload your gun. Semi-automatics should only be loaded with two shells. Keep the bolt back if you are not firing. When moving from stand five to stand one, unload the semi-automatic completely, keep the bolt back and keep the barrel raised skywards.

Guns should be broken and unloaded when moving from one trap to another. Guns should not be left unattended and they should not be left visible in locked or open cars. More people have been killed and injured by 'unloaded guns' than by loaded ones.

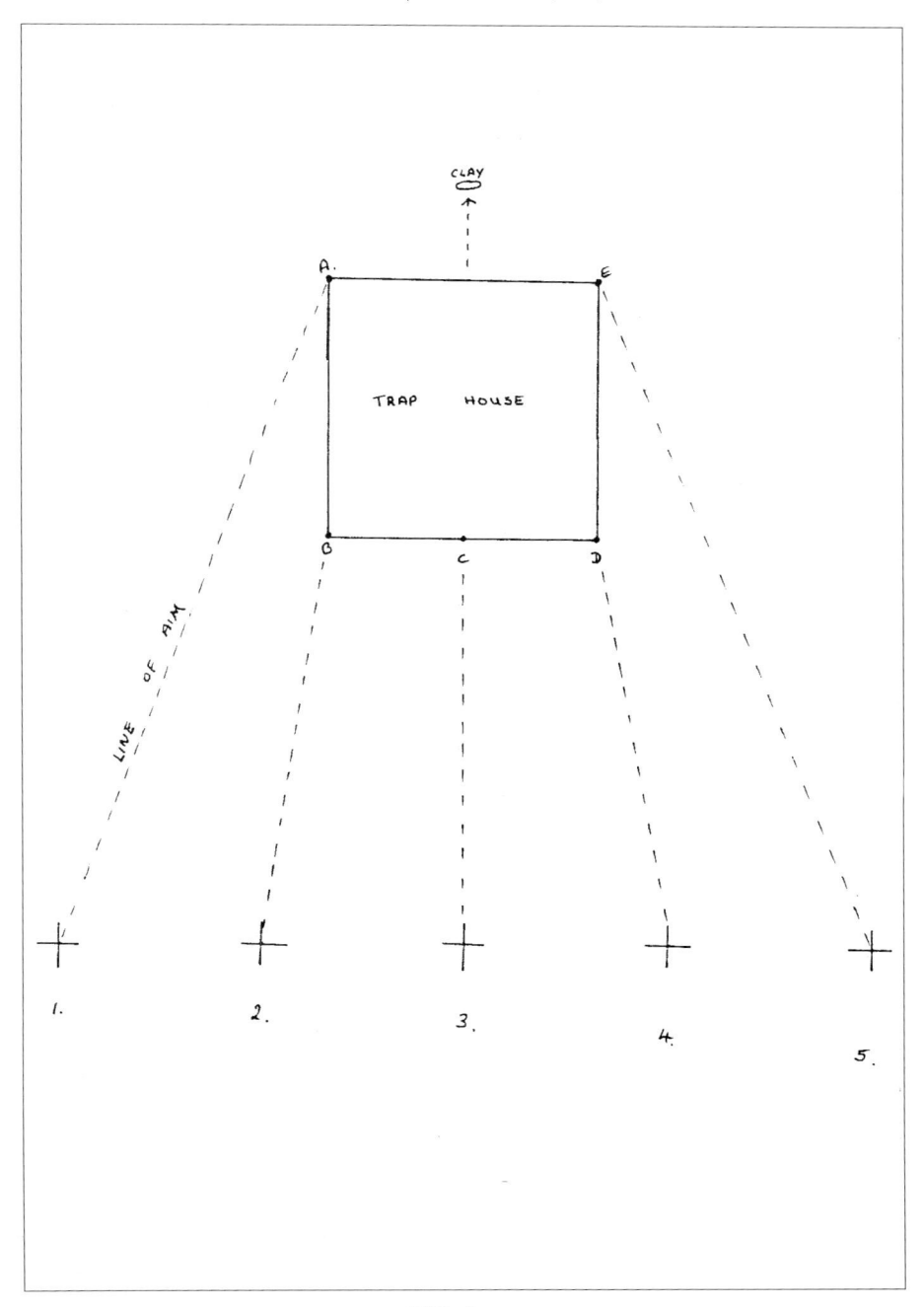

D.T.L. diagram

CHAPTER SEVENTEEN

Ruffed Grouse

The ruffed grouse is similar in size to the Irish red grouse but its markings are quite different. They are generally two colour phases: a reddish brown and grey. Their fan-like tail feathers can vary even more in colour. The males are slightly larger than the females but there are no really different distinguishing features between the sexes. The American Ruffed Grouse Society says that the best method of separating cocks from hens is to measure the tail. A mature male will have a tail feather in excess of five and seven-eights inches. A hen will have a tail less than five and one-half inches. The term ruffed came from the band of feathers which circle the base of the neck. They are a chocolate brown in colour and are seen on both males and females. During the mating season, the cock puffs out these feathers to make himself larger and attractive. He also ruffs out these feathers and expands his fan-like tail when protecting his territory.

The ruffed grouse is the most common native game bird in North America. It is found in thirty-eight of the forty-nine continental states and in all the Canadian Provinces. They range as far north as Alaska and Labrador and as far south to New Mexico. The birds have become established in places where they were not resident like Nevada and Newfoundland. The birds were introduced to these areas by releasing wild-trapped birds.

The ruffed grouse is a hardy bird which can survive hard winters which can cause the death of other species of game birds. I have shot grouse in many of the New England States but especially in Maine. Winters are long and hard in Maine and pheasants never survive through them, especially in the Northern areas. The grouse will often burrow into the snow in harsh weather to shelter from the elements. Sometimes however, the midday sun may cause the snow to melt and when the temperature drops below freezing in the afternoon, the bird may be trapped in an icy grave.

The 'fluffy partridge' as the grouse is often referred to has a varied diet which enables it to survive in many types of habitat. It is omnivorous feeding on berries, insects and green leaves. Their main diet during winter months is the buds of various trees such as birches, cherries, ironwood and aspen. At one time the ruffed grouse was put on the bounty list of animals and birds in New England as it was attacking the flower buds in the apple orchards.

If you go into an Applachian or New England wood you will hear an unusual sound like a 'constant thumping' or 'drumming'. This is the drumming display of the cock grouse on his own 'stage'. His stage is generally a log, stone or clump in the forest where he can view all potential spectators. The sound is made by beating his wings swiftly against his side and causing a vacuum. The sound has almost an automatic sense about it but it is one of the true sounds of the great American Outdoors. The grouse engages in this activity to proclaim his territory. I have never heard an Irish red grouse drumming but I have seen a cock on top of a rock which protruded from the heather. When he saw the hunters and dogs approaching, he took to flight and in many instances he took the covey with him.

The nests are made amongst dead leaves on the forest floor. The hen may lay from eight to fourteen buff coloured eggs. They hatch out after three and a half weeks and the chicks leave the nest and feed themselves as soon as they are dried off.

The population of ruffed grouse has a tendency to grow and decline in cycles. Many hunters say that it is the result of some type of parasitic worm. Another theory is that it is due to climate and the resulting supply or lack of food. Hunting by man has basically little affect on the numbers of ruffed grouse. Predators take a large number of grouse each year. Ground predators take their share but the most efficient hunters are the raptors like the horned owl and the goshawks. The loss of habitat due to the spread of urbanisation is also a significant factor. In America today, there is a great effort made to protect forests from naturally occurring fires. If forests are allowed to fully mature, they become darker and fewer middle and ground layer plants and shrubs grow. This results in loss of habitat and food for the grouse which eventually leads to a drop in numbers.

* * *

The grouse season in Maine usually runs from October 1st to 31st. As in the state of Massachusetts, hunting is not allowed on Sundays. Phil Kenny and I decided that we would travel to Secret Pond camps in Moro Plantation in Aroostook County Maine. I had been there in the past and I knew that Mark Carver who owned the camps was an excellent registered Maine Guide who put one hundred and fifty percent effort into everything he did. Phil and I didn't have any dogs as it was not feasible since we lived in Boston city. Mark had some excellent Brittany spaniels so we were hopeful that the three days we proposed to spend in Maine would be fruitful.

We loaded our gear into Phil's Jeep Cherokee pick-up. The weather was still mild in Maine so we had light shooting vests, warm woollen shirts, jeans and strong walking boots with thick socks. The gun I was going to use was my Winchester twelve gauge, National Wild Turkey Federation model with win-chokes, twenty-two inch barrel and camo-laminated stock. Phil was new to the game of shooting and hunting, so he had borrowed a single barrel hammer gun from me. The gun was of Brazilian origin with a twenty-eight inch barrel and full choke. We proposed to use No. 7 hunting grade cartridges.

The journey to Northern Maine took three and a half hours but the forests still had their beautiful fall colours. The aspen is a tree which is not native to Ireland. During the Fall in New England, the aspens display very sharp shades of red, yellow and orange which seem to light up the landscape. Traffic on the motorway was light as it was mid-week; at the week-ends many people leave the cities in order to view the spectacular display of colour. Phil was an ardent fan of Patsy Cline and between country-western music and the beautiful countryside, it seemed like only an hour before we were at our destination. The weather was still dry but we noticed the drop in temperature due to the cool fresh breeze blowing down from Canada which was only fifty to seventy miles to the North.

Secret Pond camp is self-catering so we made supper as soon as the pick-up was unloaded. Mark joined us and then we gathered around the wood stove to enquire about the hunting. He had shot a moose with one of his clients during the first week of October. It was a young bull which weighed seven hundred and fifty pounds. While out scouting for moose, they had seen good numbers of grouse so our hopes were high. From what Mark had seen, he reckoned that the birds were in one of their more bountiful cycles. We decided to begin hunting at 9.00 a.m. the following morning.

Tuesday arrived and we prepared for an active day. The weather was overcast but dry and there was a slight cool breeze. It was ideal weather for walking and for dogs to scent game. Phil filled two flasks with coffee and I made some salami and cheese sandwiches – it is very easy to burn up all your energy if you intend walking from 9.00 a.m. to 4.30 p.m.

Mark decided to head for some old abandoned farmsteads at first. The residents had left to work in the factories in the large towns and cities, and mother nature was slowly reclaiming her property with lush green undergrowth and young saplings. Mark had taken Suzie, an orange and white Brittany bitch and a young dog of the same breed whose name I cannot recall. Suzie had a bell on her collar and I explained to Phil that this was used as a locator. The brambles and shrubs are so thick that it is impossible to keep the dog in view, all the time. The 'tinkle-tinkle' of the bell tells the hunter where the dog is and when the tinkling stops, you know that the dog has come to point. I had seen Mark use the same system for hunting woodcock and I have adopted the same system for my own use in Ireland.

Five minutes into the hunt and Suzie picked up a scent. The trail got hotter and we prepared to see a plump grouse. The bitch came to point in front of me and I edged forward slipping off the safety catch on the Winchester. Instead of the beating of wings going skyward, there was a swift forward movement through the high grass. I thought it was a rabbit so I didn't fire. As it escaped into the nearby woods, I noticed that it was 'taller' than a rabbit with a brownish-white coat. Mark explained that it was a snowshoe hare which is about half the size of an Irish hare. The hind legs are very fluffy to stop the hare form sinking in the snow. The lower section of the back legs basically works as a snowshoe by spreading the weight. The hare was brown and white as it was in the middle of its colour phase. During the summer months, the hare is brown but in the depths of winter, it is snow white. The various colour phases help the hare to hide from ground predators such as bobcats and coyotes. There is often a light dusting of snow on the ground in Northern Maine in October. The brownish-white phase helps the hare to blend into its surroundings during this time. Many other animals use this method of camouflage: the stoat is another and his white pelt or ermine is very valuable.

We found no grouse at this particular farmstead so we decided to try some fields which bordered the forest. As the Brittany worked the terrain, I noticed something moving at ground level through the tall grasses. This time I knew that it was a snowshoe-hare so I covered an open section of the field where I guessed he would try to make his escape. Out he came thirty yards away and tumbled head over heels to a No. 7 cartridge. Sometimes a hare will keep running around in broad circles if he is being pursued by dogs. The Irish hare will generally make a bee-line out of an area if he is being pursued by beagles or harriers. Phil shot another hare in the same field so even if we got no grouse, we would not go hungry tonight.

We left the farms and headed for the woods where there was a good mixture of aspens, birches and ironwoods. There were blowdowns and the woods in this area were not mature. This was ideal habitat for grouse so we should at least see a few birds. Mark set the dogs to hunt on either side of the logging road and Phil and I followed behind Mark. Both dogs worked diligently and it wasn't long before Suzie set. Phil stepped up behind her as the dog held to point. At Mark's command, she pushed forward and a single grouse broke from cover. I had never seen a grouse before and Phil had never shot one. After thirty seconds, Suzie retrieved a beautiful grey phase grouse. Judging by the weight and the size, Mark said that it was a male bird.

Soon afterwards the dogs picked up another scent but before they had time to set a brace of birds vaulted skywards. I fired two shots rapidly and was lucky to down one bird. The other bird winged its way through the trees and to safety. We began to meet birds in twos and threes, and had some great sport. I could safely say that I shot on average only one out of every five birds. If a red grouse flushes on an Irish mountainside, there is only the heather to contend with or else a slight bank or ridge over which the birds will fly out of sight. In the big woods of Maine, there are trees everywhere and the ruffed grouse has a habit of flying around them. It is safe to say that we shot more trees than birds on that particular day.

We were hungry by one o'clock and stopped for lunch beside a small river. We were tired from stepping over blow-downs and the break was appreciated by both men and dogs. Mark said that he had hunted black bear in this area. Three times he had chased a large black bear to the river and each time he swam across it and the dogs had lost the trail. Mark reckoned the bear was a boar weighing about six hundred pounds. This was a huge animal when you consider that the average weight of bears in the area was two hundred pounds. A group of wood cutters passed by and stopped for a chat when they saw us. They said that they had seen grouse on a logging road which was only a half a mile away from our present location. They bid us adieu and Mark said that we would follow up their information.

The ruffed grouse like all game birds needs grit to help digest its food. The most suitable area to get grit in the Maine woods is on the gravel logging roads. The loggers would have seen the birds looking for grit especially in the afternoons. Hunters who do not have dogs or who are not fit, drive along the roads and shoot the birds when they see them. This may seem unsporting but if the birds are scarce you may have to walk many miles before you get a shot.

We proceeded to the spot the loggers mentioned and sure enough we saw some birds on the roadside. We hunted the road on either side and met about a dozen grouse. Phil got two birds and I got one. At one stage a covey of three or four birds broke wild and flew about forty yards into the trees. I followed without the dog as I had a good idea as to where they had landed. They had perched alright but it was up on the top of a tall pine tree. I knew that there was at least three birds there but all I could see was one. I shouted and circled the tree a few times but to no avail. The birds weren't going to take to flight and as far as they were concerned, I was as dangerous as any coyote or bobcat.

The light was fading at 4.30 p.m. so we decided to head back for camp. The dogs were tired and our calf muscles were beginning to ache from the exertions of the day. As we drove along the odd grouse appeared on the roadside searching for grit. The white-tail deer were moving to feeding areas but all we saw was their white flags as they bolted into cover. We had one day down and two more to go. All we needed now was a good night's rest and a hearty meal to prepare for what was a thoroughly enjoyable upland game hunt.

CHAPTER EIGHTEEN

Wild Turkey

When the average person in the street thinks of Christmas, thoughts turn to Christmas fare and eating turkey. The majority of people, north and south of the equator, eat turkey with cranberry sauce on 25th December. However, turkey became the main item on the menu after the Mayflower with the Pilgrim Fathers landed on Plymouth Rock on Cape Cod, Massachusetts.

The Irish ate goose for their Christmas dinner. The gentry or royalty in England ate peacock or royal swan. The pilgrims were not prepared for their first winter in Massachusetts. They were supposed to land further south near Virginia but the powers in higher authority wanted to plant the land further north. The pilgrims would have died during the first winter except that the local Indians took pity on them and provided corn, pumpkin and the local wild bird – turkey.

Americans celebrate this occasion every year on the last Thursday in November – Thanksgiving. To an American, Thanksgiving is almost as important as Christmas. Cranberry sauce comes from the cranberry which is harvested in the bogs of Southern Massachusetts.

Turkeys were prevalent all along the eastern sea board of the United States. In the 1800's the early settlers shot and sold them by the cart load. By the beginning of this century, the Eastern turkey was almost wiped out and eventually a moratorium was put on hunting.

The Massachusetts Department of Fisheries and Wildlife did a lot of research and ground work into bringing back the wild turkey. Adult birds were taken from other states and released into the wild. Eventually the birds took hold and began to reproduce. After a number of years, there was sufficient game to introduce hunting again.

In order to hunt turkey in Massachusetts today, a hunter needs a game hunting licence and you also have to apply for a turkey tag. There is a Spring hunting season which lasts for about two weeks in May. Cocks, Toms or Gobblers as they are called, can be shot at this time – no hens. Hens may be shot during the fall season. Young cocks or jakes can also be shot during Spring. The hunting method completely prohibits the use of dogs. You can use a bow and arrow, musket or shotgun. The most common weapon used is a twelve or ten bore shotgun. The gun may have a twenty-two inch barrel and may be completely painted in camouflage or the stock and forearm grip may be made from camo-laminated wood. Three inch, No. 4 copper plated magnum cartridges are generally used. Turkeys are shot in the neck so it is important to have a hard hitting and penetrating pellet.

The gobbler is very territorial and aggressive during the mating season which occurs in May. He has an excellent sense of hearing and sight. His sense of smell is his only weak point. The hunter doesn't go to the turkey but the turkey comes to the hunter. In order to do this, the hunter must be an excellent caller or else use turkey calling equipment which gives him or her the advantage. The professional turkey callers use a type of plastic semi-circular diaphragm which fits in the mouth. I could never master this method as I found myself almost choking on the foreign object in my mouth. I used a H.S. Strut box caller. By moving the wooden handle on one side, I could imitate the sounds of another gobbler. When I scraped the handle on the other side of the box, I could make the sounds of an old boss hen. Every aspect of the gobblers breeding character was covered by using this method.

Turkey hunters are the masters when it comes to camouflaging themselves. Not a hair is left visible. When you hunt turkey, you sit on the ground at the base of tree and call your quarry in. The face is always heavily painted or some type of mask is worn. Gloves are worn or the hands may also be painted brown, green or black. The barrel of the shotgun is generally matte finished so that there will be no chance of sunlight reflecting and alerting the bird. Turkey hunters are so good at hiding themselves and calling, that they are often mistaken for turkeys by other hunters. A good trunk of a tree is the best protection from another hunter who may come in from behind. At least if the other hunter is approaching from your vanguard, you will see him.

My friend, Barry, and I decided to go to the Berkshires in Western Massachusetts on the border with New York to shoot turkey. Barry knew where there were some big Toms but more importantly he had permission to hunt on private land from a number of landowners. There was a lot of public or state land available for hunting but this would be under heavy pressure on the first day of the season. I packed my gear and fishing rods as we were going on a Sunday and there is no hunting in Massachusetts on Sundays.

I drove from Boston and met Barry near South Yarmouth. We put all the gear into his Ford pick-up and set forth for the Berkshires which were almost three and a half hours drive. The weather was dry, sunny and warm.

There was no breeze which should also help the hunting. I was very excited as I had never hunted in that area before. I had been skiing on Brodie Mountain the previous March but I saw no turkeys on that occasion.

We booked into the local motel and were lucky to get the last room in the town. There was a lot of other hunters who had the same plans for tomorrow as we did. Barry drove ten miles to scout one of the farms where he had permission to shoot. The farm was down in a valley and the fields bordered the woods. It was 4.30 p.m. but we could see three large toms strutting about in one of the fields. Prospects for tomorrow were certainly looking good!

We drove down to a creek at the base of the fields and decided to go fishing for brook trout. I had my fly rod and I put on two wet flies – a Tups Indispensible and an Alexander. I caught three small brookies and lost a number more. Barry had caught eight when I met him. He was using small lizards or salamanders as bait which he found under the stones on the bank of the stream. I decided to try this method. The salamanders were placed on the fly hook and I soon had half a dozen brookies. We lit a fire and roasted the trout whole. They were small but tasty. After washing them down with a couple of beers it was time to pin-point the turkeys for tomorrow and to find a suitable area to call them in.

In order to locate a turkey, you use a small call which irritates him and causes him to gobble. We had owl hooters. An owl hooter simulates the call of an owl; the sound of which annoys the turkey. We located two turkeys by this means and found a suitable tree on the side of a track with enough cover for a hunter but also with a clear enough view for a shot. The turkey would have to come within thirty yards for a safe shot. I hooted on another suitable trail where wild raspberry plants were growing. A raccoon appeared on the scene after five minutes, scented me after coming within twenty-five yards and then went foraging in another direction. We had enough knowledge gathered at this stage so we drove back to the motel as we would have to be up two hours before dawn in order to be in position before the turkeys left their roosts.

It was an hour before sunrise as we entered the woods. We moved slowly and silently so as not to disturb any of the woodland inhabitants. Barry and I split up and went our separate ways. I hadn't heard or seen any other hunters so I was quietly confident. Fifteen minutes later I was seated with my back to the tree which I had chosen the previous evening. As my breathing returned to its normal rhythm, I waited for the sun to rise.

Just before dawn broke, a herd of five white-tail deer passed about fifty yards to my right. They were probably returning from grazing on the pasture land. Soon after I heard a turkey preparing to leave his roost so I got ready to call him in. After twenty minutes he was out in front of me at a distance of one hundred yards. I gave a few clucks and purrs on the wooden box call and after every three to five minutes, he would call back. He was approaching slowly and carefully. Turkeys are very cautious in woodland as they are always waiting for a coyote or some other predator to jump on them. Turkeys feel more at ease strutting in green fields where they can see every movement. Old gobblers did not grow elderly and wise by running into investigate every sound they heard in the forests. A young gobbler or jake as he is called, may be less suspicious and this is the reason why many of them are killed.

I could now see a fine gobbler approaching through a trail about forty yards out. I made a few more clucks and purrs and then slowly put down the box and raised my twelve gauge. It was a Winchester 1100 pump action with a camo-laminated stock and grip. The barrel was twenty-two inches long with a one-quarter win-choke fitted. It could fire three inch magnums as well as steel shot. The short dull-matte finished barrel made it ideal for such situations. I put the front bead on his neck, slipped off the safety and prepared to fire. At that precise instant a shot thundered below me on the hill. My tom cocked his head, turned and exited the area as fast as fork lightning. I waited another two hours but nothing called or nothing approached the area. It was not 9.30 a.m. and time to call it a day.

I made my way back quietly so as not to disturb Barry in case he was still hunting. There were no turkey calls coming from his area so I presumed that he must have returned to the pickup. Sure enough he was there with a fine bronze gobbler. The shot I heard was his and the turkey complied with all his plans. He didn't see or hear any other turkeys all morning.

We took the bird to the registration station. He weighed twenty-two pounds and had a six inch beard growing from his chest. The beard consists of long black fibres or strings. The older the bird the longer the beard. We saw a number of other gobblers which weighed about fourteen pounds on average. I wasn't disappointed as we headed back that afternoon for Boston. On another trip I would get one of twenty-two pounds with a compound bow in Pennsylvania.

To Hunt, Shoot and Stalk

Fully mounted Tom Bobcat (Chapter 14)

Bobcat taken with handgun (Chapter 13)

To Hunt, Shoot and Stalk

A Scottish deer-stalker with traditional Sherlock Holmes headgear (Chapter 15)

Lodgings for the rambler in the Highlands (Chapter 15)

A Ruffed Grouse on his drumming log (Chapter 17)

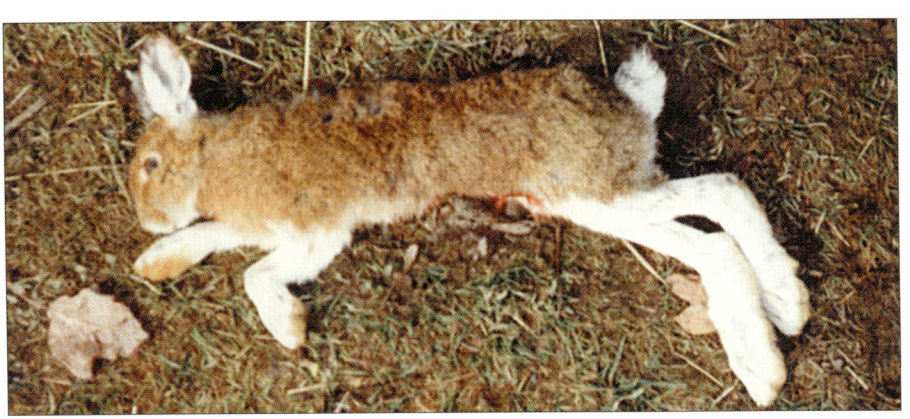

Snoeshoe Hare at half-way stage in colour change (Chapter 17)

TO HUNT, SHOOT AND STALK

Doug with a 22lb Spring Gobbler (Chapter 18)

Jared with a Fall Gobbler (Chapter 18)

CHAPTER NINETEEN

Bear in Maine : Treestands

Hunting bear from treestands is the most common method used by hunters. It is less expensive than using hounds and not as much equipment is needed. It is legal in most states and provinces in the U.S. and Canada whereas hunting with dogs is being curtailed or banned in many areas. Permission must be sought from the local forestry company or landowners. Customised or home-made stands may be used.

Homemade stands are basically made of pieces of 2X4 nailed together and then nailed to a tree. It is extremely important to remove all the nails when the stand is taken down. A nail hitting the blade of a saw has the potential to cause serious mechanical damage and personal injury.

A tree stand basically comprises of a ladder measuring 15-20 feet and a platform coming out at right angles from the tree. The stand may be located at a crossing point on an animal trail or in a specific area, which has been baited by the hunter. Some hunters used to locate their stands near refuse dumps where bears were known to forage but this has been banned by many local authorities.

Ron who was staying in camp with me hoped to take a bear from a tree stand. The average shot taken from such a position would range at 25 yards at most. However a certain allowance would have to be made for the fact that the shot is always taken downwards from a tree stand. Ron practised everyday with his trusty blackpowder muzzle loader. Standing at 25 paces he could always put the ball in a 2' circle. The barrel was very long and as far as I could remember it was at least 38'.

There was always a huge cloud of smoke from both the muzzle and from the flint and pan. I fired a shot from the gun at one stage. It must have taken 2-3 seconds from the time I pulled the trigger to when the flint ignited the power in the pan, to the flash in the pan igniting the power in the barrel. The flash in the pan can cause an inexperienced hunter to flinch and to throw the shot. After the shot has been taken the hunter has to wait for the cloud of smoke to disappear to see if the target has been struck. This is fine in the case of a paper target but it is troublesome if the quarry is an animal, which may not be accurately dispatched. Ron was completely at home with his weapon however. He told me that the Americans used this type of weapon during the War of Independence in 1770's. The farmers used the .50 calibre as their hunting rifle and military rifle. The bullet or ball was about the size of a large ball bearing. I certainly would not like to be the person who was on the receiving end.

The ideal time to hunt bear from a treestand is early in the morning or late in the evening when the air is cool and the bears are most active. Ron liked to rest in the morning and in the week that we hunted together he never once went out at dawn. Mark told Ron to wear camouflage gear and to either use camo-paint or a mask on his face. Ron wouldn't hear of this. He wore a red shirt, jeans and a peaked hat any time he sat in a stand. The long barrelled musket always rested across his lap.

Mark took Ron to an active bear bait the evening after I had got my bear. I had to stay in the truck, as we didn't want to have too much human scent in the area. When you go up in a bear stand you should have your gun, insect repellent, a candy bar and a good cushion. An empty plastic bottle with a screw-on cap is also required. You cannot expect any animal to come to an area, which has been marked by man! We left the area and Mark said that he would collect Ron in three hours.

Coyotes often visit bear bait. I had filled my bear tag so I was ineligible until the next season. Coyotes can be shot all year round so I decided that I would try and get one or more if I was lucky. A friend of Mark's had waited for bear in a particular stand the week before and a pack of fourteen coyotes came in. He was so frightened that he got down from the stand and left the area. This was a dangerous thing to do, not because the Coyotes might attack but because he could have got lost or hurt in the vast forests. The forests are almost the size of Ireland and in some areas there may be no inhabitants for ten to fifteen miles.

I had all my camo gear on as well as having my face painted. I had put on insect repellent as the bite from a female mosquito is very irritating especially when you have to stay still for long periods of time. Mark said that he would come back for me in two and a half hours. It was now six p.m.

The only sounds I could hear were woodpeckers and the odd moose. As the evening wore on the lonesome call of the loon could be heard from a distant lake. The Loon is a solitary water bird, black and white in colour with a long pointed beak for catching fish. When you hear the call of the Loon you know that you are in a true wilderness area. The eerie call of the Loon is slowly disappearing which reflects the advance of man into the wild natural ecosystems.

The first indication a hunter receives of an animal's approach is the rustle of a leaf. The story goes in Maine of many hunters hearing such a sound and then seeing a deer or bear approach. However other hunters tell of the bear being scared away by a low flying jet on a practice run from an airforce base. Some of the locals say that cruise missiles are test flown over the forests of Maine. Wary animals will not approach bait under such circumstances. The only animals that came near my stand were small red squirrels. I heard no shots in the distance even though I knew that other bear hunters were in their stands. It was 9 p.m., too dark to shoot legally and yet there was no sign of Mark and the pick-up.

Thirty minutes later I heard the Chevy rumbling down the logging road. I got down from the stand and walked one hundred yards towards the sound of the running engine. I presumed they had been delayed because Ron had shot a bear. Ron had shot at a big bruin but as yet he had not retrieved it.

Apparently Ron saw the bear approaching and the bear also spotted Ron in his treestand. Wild animals like deer and bear generally do not look up as danger never comes from that direction. Predators, which they encounter always, hunt at ground level. Maybe it was Ron's face, which caught the bear's attention. Both hunter and quarry eyed themselves for a few moments. The .50 calibre was lying across his thighs so Ron could not make any sudden movement without alarming the bear. He would have to swing the gun through a wide arc of 90 degrees to bring the sights on his target.

Suddenly the bear must have realised that the strange face in the tree belonged to a man. The bear turned about to flee and as he did so Ron swung the gun into position and fired as the Bruin disappeared into the bush. Ron was sure that he hit the animal but he did not leave the stand, as it was too dangerous to do so. He waited for Mark but at that stage it was too dark to see anything.

Ron had helped me to drag out my bear so I owed him a favour. I said that we would all go back and search with torches for the animal. Ron was such a good shot that the bear was probably dead in the heavy undergrowth. Mark's reply was 'No-way!' The most dangerous animal in the Maine woods is an injured bear or a bear with cubs. If we came across the bear and he wasn't dead the results would be catastrophic. Under no circumstances would we attempt to track down the bear tonight. We would wait for first light in the morning.

Next day we loaded our rifles, and a shotgun into the Chevy. The shotgun, as always, is an ideal gun in a precarious situation. Mark also had his leather holster with the .44 magnum. I cannot recall bringing any dog. We would probably find the bear dead or else follow the blood trail on foot.

When we arrived at the stand Mark led the way cautiously while we followed. He checked the general area and then Ron and I moved in. There was no sign of the bear or a blood trail. Ron went to the stand and walked to the spot where he had fired at the bear – no blood, hair or drag marks. After a few moments examining the track Ron found the answer to all his questions. Lying at the side of the well worn trail was a rock about the size of an American football. A chunk the size of a golfball had been blown out of it. It was a clean miss and the bear would probably live till next season. There was no way that such a bear would come near a bait or treestand in the near future.

Ron was disappointed but he was glad that the bear was not injured or wounded. He went out every evening for the rest of the week but his luck was not in. I waited in a tree stand for Coyotes again and my lotto numbers came up but not in the right order. Two evenings later I was up in a different treestand. There was a clearing of about 200 yards in diameter in front of me. A trail led into the clearing from the North. There was no wind or breeze so I would not be detected and I should also be able to hear the slightest sound. The undergrowth consisted of four-foot high trees and shrubs. Plenty of cover for a cautious bear or Coyote to make their approach. I had the .3030 rested across my knees and if I did move my head I did so in slow motion – quick or sudden movements are the ones which alert and frighten animals. I heard a rustle in the dry leaves behind my stand. My heart began to pound with excitement, as I was sure it was a deer. Deer season hadn't opened yet but it would be nice to observe a fine buck from such a position. I couldn't turn around and yet the rustling continued. Eventually I turned around slowly and there was my buck – a red squirrel rummaging in the leaves for food.

Forty minutes passed with neither sight nor sound of anything. The odd mosquito flew in front of my face but the Musk repellent kept them at bay. It is so powerful that the solution can take the dye out of some objects. Suddenly I saw a Coyote's ear twitch down the trail. The animal was forty yards out and coming straight towards me. He was moving through the undergrowth so I swung the rifle to my shoulder and cocked the hammer. I rested my left forearm on my left knee and aimed at the spot where the trail entered the clearing. I waited for almost five minutes but nothing appeared.

Had I being imagining things? Sitting in the one position for hours and looking at the same inanimate objects enables the human eye and brain to put movement where there is none. Suddenly I saw a big black object ten yards from the clearing. It was a large black bear who was slowly making her way towards the bait. Eventually the sow entered the clearing, looked everywhere before taking a slice of bread from the bait. She took one bite and crossed the clearing towards the ladder of my stand. My heart was in my mouth, as I knew that black bears have no problem climbing trees; never mind going up ladders. I had the sights placed right between the middle of her small beady eyes. My bear tag was filled but if she came up the fifteen feet to me there was only one solution to the problem. She stopped at the bottom of the ladder, sniffed carefully but NEVER looked up. Obviously the bear didn't know that I was there. She moved back to the bait, sat down for thirty seconds, took a bite from a piece of bread and disappeared as quietly as she had arrived. Bears may be big and black but they move without a sound and their black coat doesn't always given their presence away. I still regret not having a video camera with me on the occasion. The bear never came back that evening and I never saw a Coyote for the remainder of the week.

I stated that the bear was a sow or female. She had no cubs with her. True sportsmen do not shoot bears with cubs. I told Mark what had happened. He wrote to me at Christmas saying that a friend of his went to the same tree stand two weeks later. A large bear came in during the evening and he shot it with one shot from a 30.06. It was a black female which weighed 285 lbs.

CHAPTER TWENTY

Dogs

A dog is a man's best friend, but for the hunter it is essential in order to find game and to retrieve game. Dogs can be divided into two basic categories for the game shooter – pointing/setting dogs and flushers/retrievers.

The pointing or setting dogs were originally used by people who practised falconry. The dogs often hunted in pairs, set or pointed the birds on the ground and when the quarry was flushed, the falcon was released to kill the bird, or rabbit. Some types of setter/pointer dogs also retrieve the bird when shot. The English pointer, the English setter, the Llewllyn and the Irish setter, are the most common types used in Ireland. These breeds are very suitable for hunting grouse on open mountain as they can cover a lot of ground and are clearly visible due to their size. Most of the breeds mentioned will retrieve shot birds but some individual dogs will not. When buying a pup of these breeds, you must take into consideration that the dog may not begin to work on average until it is $1\frac{1}{2}$ years old. The pointers and setters are ideal for hunting in beet and stubble fields. However, when birds become wary and head for heavy or dense cover, these dogs are at a disadvantage as many do not like to penetrate such obstacles. Setters and pointers of the breeds mentioned are not suitable for duck shooting and wild-fowling.

The most popular dog for the ordinary shooter is the English springer spaniel or more commonly known as the springer spaniel. There are many types of spaniel and as the name implies, their ancestors came from Spain. The springer is either black and white, or liver and white in colour. It is on average 50 cms high at the shoulder, curly, floppy ears and a short to a three-quarter length tail. The springer has a friendly energetic temperament. It is the basic flushing/retrieving dog but needs to be taught to strictly obey all commands. The springer is also a very gentle dog where children are concerned.

The springer will hunt ditches, hedgerows and all types of cover. When he picks up a scent his tail will begin to wag swiftly. When he comes up to the pheasant, woodcock or rabbit, he will flush it, so it is vitally important to have the dog working within shotgun range. When the quarry is shot, the dog will bring it back to hand or else will hunt the wounded quarry until it is found. Springer spaniels will be ready for the field at one year old and sometimes even earlier. A pure bred pup may cost on average eighty pounds whereas a registered dog may cost from one hundred and twenty to one hundred and eighty pounds. No matter how well bred a dog is, you take your chance when buying any puppy.

Springer spaniels love water. It is important for the condition of their coat that they enter water at least once a week. They are fearless in the water and do not hesitate to retrieve any wild fowl no matter what the weather conditions. I have seen them to cross flooded rivers to retrieve duck and to be carried one hundred yards downstream by the current. When the winters were colder in Ireland, I saw springers retrieving mallard across flooded bogs where the ice was two inches thick. Since the springer is so energetic, playful and hyper-active, it is important that the dog should drop to the whistle or drop to shot. There is nothing more frustrating than to sprint after a racing springer and to see a fine cock pheasant flush forty to sixty yards out of range. Springers are not the greatest of watchdogs and many a hunter has 'lost' a springer due to the dog's willingness to take a lift from any prospective thief.

The springer spaniel is often seen on driven shoots in association with the labrador. The labrador has its origins on the east coast of Canada, New Foundland and Labrador, where it was used by the fishermen to retrieve items of netting and the odd fisherman who fell overboard. Its physique made it impervious to the cold water temperatures. The labrador is used on the driven shoots to pick up dead and wounded game – not to drive the game. The wild-fowler will use the 'Lab' to fetch dead and wounded birds from teal to geese. The most popular colour is black. Labradors also come in yellow (gold). In the U.S. on the east coast, the most popular colour seems to be chocolate.

In recent times there has been a lot of attention paid to HPRs. These dogs are dual purpose as they hunt, point and retrieve. The HPR which most hunters have heard of or used is the German pointer. Not alone will this dog set a grouse but he will also retrieve a duck from water. The H.P.R. can be a great advantage for the hunter who has little space or time and needs an all-purpose dog.

I used springer spaniels but now I use a HPR called the Brittany Spaniel. The ancestory of the brittany spaniel can be traced to France and England. The story says that English men went to Brittany and brought their Llewllyn setters with them. For some reason or other, they kennelled their setters for the year in Brittany, the Breton's spaniel inter-bred with the setters, so you got a setting spaniel who has the talents of both breeds.

The Brittany comes in three colour phases: orange and white; tri-colour; and, liver and white. Generally speaking it has no tail or just a small butt. It is more angular at the shoulder than the English springer, and of a lighter build. It is an extremely fit dog and can keep going all day. On the other hand, he is hyper-active and bold and must be kept under strict control.

I have my third Brittany spaniel who was only ten months when he was taken out shooting duck on the 1st September 1998. He retrieved eight mallard and one teal. Three weeks into September, he set and retrieved his first cock-grouse. At the end of the 1998/99 season, he had set and retrieved pheasants, woodcock and snipe from beet fields, forests, ditches and bogs. On one occasion, he found and set a wounded deer. A Brittany pup can cost one hundred and fifty to one hundred and seventy-five pounds, and they generally begin to work best from their second hunting season. When the 'Britt' comes out of water he may look extremely thin but this is the dog's physique. I have found that a Brittany spaniel will retrieve a dummy once to hand but not to hand the second time – they like the real item, not a substitute. I think that this is a sign of the dog's great intelligence.

Andy Hickey, who has trained dogs for Dr. patrick Hillery, former President of the Irish Republic, compares a dog to a car. The steering is for turning the dog left or right or to quarter. The brakes are for stopping the dog. There are three gears: neutral, forward and reverse. Neutral is for walking the dog quietly to heel. Forward is to go out, hunt or retrieve. Reverse is to recall the dog. The dog, just like a car, has to stop before it can change into a different motion or gear.

There are many books written about gundogs and training. Videos on gundog training are very popular at the moment. If a novice hunter wishes to purchase or train a dog he or she should contact the 'local expert' first as his advice is probably gained from long hard years of experience. After careful consideration you should then decide on what breed of dog is most suitable for the type of game you hunt and the terrain in which you will conduct your particular brand of the sport. Professional trainers do an excellent job on preparing young dogs but there is also great satisfaction to be gained from training your own pup.

To Hunt, Shoot and Stalk

Eoin Lalor (R.I.P.), the author's father with his Springer Spaniels

CHAPTER TWENTY-ONE

Firearm Legislation

There are approximately two hundred thousand (200,000) licensed firearms in the Republic of Ireland. Over ninety percent of these guns are shotguns and rifles as handguns are basically illegal in the twenty-six counties. The vast majority of the shotguns would be used for hunting and clay pigeon shooting. The rifles would be used for rabbits, foxes and deer. There is a lot of controversy in the United States at the moment with regard to gun ownership and gun control. The 'right to bear arms', which is written into the Constitution of the U.S., is one of the most protected rights of the American citizen. Each of the fifty states has its own local gun laws whereas in Ireland the law is the same throughout the country. The local Garda Superintendent has a major input into who may be granted a firearms licence.

There are certain procedures to be followed when applying for a firearms certificate or licence. There are ten classes of firearm certificates which are currently issued namely:

1. Unlimited shotgun (i.e. first shotgun)..£20.00
2. Second or subsequent shotgun...£ 5.00
   (must be a holder of an unlimited certificate)
3. Limited shotgun..£ 5.00
   (e.g. granted to farmers/landowners for vermin control)
4. Rifle..£30.00
5. Airgun and air rifle..£30.00
6. Crossbow...£20.00
   (availability and possession confined to responsible persons who can establish a reason for having them for a legitimate sporting and recreational use)
7. Humane killer..£13.00
8. Prohibited weapon (e.g. ringmaster at circus –
   tranquiliser, prop in play)..£ 5.00
9. Northern Ireland Firearms Licence (apply to Royal Ulster Constabulary)
10. European licence

How to apply for a Firearms Certificate

1. Applicant must obtain a Bill of Sale (from the vendor) and present it at his local Garda Station at which he made application on a Form PC20.
2. If the firearm is a shotgun and he wishes to shoot birds and hares in the open season, he completes Form DHL 1 (Section 24 and 25, 1976 Wildlife Act)
3. (a) Written nomination from 2 landowners is required for a Limited Certificate where the applicant does not have land of his own, unless the nominator is a substantial landowner.
    (b) Section 28 of the 1976 Wildlife Act states that before a person is entitled to hunt 'Game' birds or protected wild animals, that person must be qualified. In order to qualify, a person must be at least sixteen years of age and:
    1) be entitled to sporting rights over the land; or
    2) be the guest, invitee, servant or agent, or possess the written authority of a person who is entitled to the sporting rights over the land; or
    3) be a member of a body of persons (e.g. Gun Club, Game Protection Association, etc.) which is entitled to sporting rights over the land or which has such authority.

    Note:: that a member of a Gun Club or Game Protection Association etc. does not require to have written permission but the Club must have authority to hunt on the lands. It should be noted that 'Sporting Rights' does not include 'Fishing Rights'. Non residents should apply to the Minister for Justice, C/O Department of Justice, St. Stephen's Green, Dublin 2, Ireland.
4. Garda, after checking the form completes the back of Form PC20 for a favourable report. to the Superintendent. If the position is otherwise, a report on separate paper will be submitted.
5. Superintendent will signify his intention to issue a certificate on back of Form PC20 (Certificate may issue). Forward certificate for signature and appropriate fee. Completed Form PC20 forwarded by Superintendent to Firearms Computer Section and assigned a computer number and returned
    1) The fee is collected from the applicant and a certificate prepared in (3) triplicate using the computer record number
    2) The certificate and first copy will be removed from the book and sent to the Superintendent with the fee, Fee Summary Form and PC20
    3) Receipt may be detached from original certificate and given to the applicant Two or more persons may hold Firearms Certificates in respect of the same weapon.

Persons disentitled to hold Firearms Certificates (Section 8 of the Act of 1925 as amended by Section 17 of Firearms Act, 1964)

The following are disentitled to hold a firearm certificate, namely, any person:
1. under the age of 16 years
2. of intemperate habits
3. of unsound mind
4. sentenced in this country to penal servitude for any term which has not expired or which has expired within the previous five years for a crime in the course of which
   (a) a firearm was used or a firearm or imitation firearm was produced to intimidate any person, or
   (b) a threat to use a firearm against any person or property was made.
5. sentenced in this country to penal servitude or imprisonment for any term of not less than three months which has not expired or has expired within the previous five years for a crime consisting of or including an assault on any person
6. who is subject to police supervision
7. who is bound by recognisance to keep the peace and be of good behaviour a condition of which is that such person shall not have in his possession or use or carry any firearm or ammunition

Procedure for applying for a licence in respect of a heavy calibre rifle

The procedure for obtaining a rifle certificate in respect of a heavy calibre rifle is relatively simple:
1. The applicant must first of all be in possession of a recently dated letter of permission from the landowner
2. He will then forward this letter, together with details of his firearm, to Dúchas, The Heritage Service, in order to obtain a hunting licence. He must also supply details of the Folio No. or Land Certificate No. of land the applicant wishes to shoot on. He must also give the calibre and make of the firearm and the weight of the bullet he intends using.
3. Dúchas will then consider the application and, if approved, will issue a hunting licence to the applicant.
4. The applicant will then call to his/her local Garda Station with the hunting licence, together with the permission from the landowner. An Application Form (PC20) is completed in respect of the application for a rifle licence and he signs same.
5. The application is then forwarded to the District Officer who will in turn forward same to the Crime Pevention Officer for report. The C.P.O. will confine his report to the security aspect of the storage of the firearm and he will confirm that a security cabinet has been installed at the residence of the applicant.

Firearms Certificates for heavy calibre rifles i.e. deer rifles

The new regulations in relation to the granting of licences for heavy calibre rifles came into operation on the 1st December 1991. The conditions are set out as follows:

1. That the Superintendent where the applicant resides must be satisfied that Section 4 of the Firearms Act 1925 must be complied with.
2. That the applicant is in possession of a hunting licence granted by the Minister for Arts, Heritage, Gaeltacht and The Islands, under Section 29(1) of the Wildlife Act, 1976.
3. That the storage and security of the firearm is the responsibility of the holder. He should, prior to issuing of the licence, provide in his place of residence a strong cabinet where the firearm can be stored.
4. When in use the licence holder should take all reasonable steps to ensure the safety and security of the weapon.
5. The calibre of a deer rifle must not be less than .22/250 or more than .270 inches. The bullet must be at least 55 grains in weight.(Wildlife Act)

European Firearms Pass

The European Firearms Pass is a passport like booklet which is issued by the relevant authority of a member State to the holder of a lawfully held firearm. It is valid for the period of validity of his Firearms Certificate and is renewed each year with his/her gun license for up to 5 years MAX. The European Firearms Pass is a non-transferrable document on which the details of the firearm in the possession of the holder are inserted. The pass must always be in the possession of the holder when using the firearm.

In this country an application for a European Firearms Pass is made directly to the Superintendent of the Garda Síochana for the District in which the applicant resides only. The Superintendent will notify Crime and Security Branch and request a blank European Firearms Pass.

The Firearms Pass enables the holder to travel to another member State with the firearm to which the pass refers. However, where a firearm cannot be transferred to another member State without the prior consent of that State, the person concerned must obtain the consent from that State. This can be obtained on Form ECFA/C. Certain restrictions apply in respect of some European countries. For example, a person wishing to hunt in France must have an invitation from his host together with a Firearms Pass prior to obtaining consent from that State. Where prior consent is not required by a member State, a hunter or marksman can travel to that country if he is in possession of a current Firearms Pass.

A European Firearms Pass is accepted in Northern Ireland with a visitors certificate from the RUC.

Security, storage and maintenance of legally held firearms
(Guidelines issued by an Garda Síochana)

Approximately 200,000 firearms are issued in this country. Regrettably accidents involving legally held firearms are common. Between 1980 and 1990 almost eighty people were killed as a result of the accidental discharge of legally held firearms. The need to re-emphasise the causes of such accidents is self-evident. One life lost is one too many.

Use / handling of firearms
Do:
1. Always treat as being loaded until the contrary is proven.
2. Always unload when not in use and carry firearm with action open.
3. Always prove i.e. break open and inspect for loaded ammunition when picked up.
4. Carry with the safety catch on especially on sporting occasions.
5. Use only ammunition recommended by manufacturers.

Do Not:
1. Handle carelessly or unnecessarily point or aim.
2. Load until ready to use.
3. Place a finger inside the trigger guard until it is intended to snap, practice or fire.

Maintenance
1. Before use for the current season have the weapon inspected by a gunsmith or other competent person to ensure that it is free of defect, is serviceable and safe.
2. Clean thoroughly after use on each occasion, as recommended by manufacturer.

Security and Storage
Do:
1. Dismantle when not in use. Remove rifle bolts and break shotguns into component parts.
2. Store parts of weapons separately in secure places.
3. Avail of any safe storage facility provided by firearms dealers. (Better again, get your own gun-safe).
4. When advertising for sale, use a box number.

Do Not:
1. Use an address or telephone number when advertising for sale.

Applying for a Licence in Northern Ireland

Application forms for the grant of a Firearm Certificate are available from all local Police Stations, Registered Firearms Dealers and Firearms Clubs. A Firearm Certificate is valid for three years.

To avoid delays in processing an application, it is very important that all of the questions are answered fully and properly and the application is signed. If a particular item does not apply please state NOT APPLICABLE. Once completed, your application should be taken to your local Police Station, accompanied by the following:

- Two recent passport sized photographs, face without a hat, 45 mm x 35 mm, properly endorsed (see application form for details).
- The correct fee – cash or cheque/postal order made payable to 'PANI'.
- Letters of permission to shoot on land (when applicable).
- Proof of club membership (when applicable).
- Either (a) if acquiring from a registered firearms dealer, a bill of sale; or (b) if acquiring from another Firearm Certificate holder, a letter of authority, the seller's Firearm Certificate and a completed Form 30(1)(b).

As we go to print there are Amendments to the 1976 Wildlife Act which as of now have not been passed into law.

Bibliography

HUNTING IN IRELAND by Colin A. Lewis.
..........................Published by J.A. Allen & Co.

BAILEY'S HUNTING DIRECTORY, 1995-'96.

TEN GREAT IRISH HUNTS by Mike MacEwan.
..........................Published by Punchestown Books.

HISTORY OF FOX HUNTING by Roger Longrigg.
..........................Published by Macmillan London Ltd.

THE YEAR ROUND by Guy Wheeler.
..........................Published by Gentry Books.

THE HUNTING YEAR by Alison Guest and Tony Jackson.
..........................Published by Jenkins, Barrie Ltd.

THE N.A.R.G.C. – A PROFILE
..........................Sureprint (Clonmel) Ltd.

LAND MAMMALS OF IRELAND – FOREST AND WILDLIFE SERVICE
..........................Designed, Produced by Q.M.A. Ltd.

DONERAILE FOREST PARK – FOREST AND WILDLIFE SERVICE
.... Printed by Colorprint Ltd.

LIVESTOCK ON THE FARM by Prof. C.Byrner Jones
..........................The Gresham Publishing Co. Ltd.

IRISH FIELD MONUMENTS – NATIONAL PARKS AND MONUMENTS SERVICE
..........................Issued by the Commissioners of Public Works

WILDLIFE EXPLORER
..........................International Masters Publishers Ltd.

OUT AND ABOUT - EAMON DE BUITLÈAR
..........................Published by Gill and Macmillan

THE NATIONAL WILD TURKEY FEDERATION OF AMERICA

THE NATIONAL RIFLE ASSOCIATION OF AMERICA